WHAT YOU SHOULD KNOW ABOUT

ANTI-BRIBERY COMPLIANCE

EDITED BY ALEXANDRA WRAGE
& ROBERT CLARK

ISBN-13: 978-1542657594
ISBN-10: 1542657598

Acknowledgments

The editors acknowledge with gratitude the substantial contributions to this book by Tom Hoskins, Jessica Tillipman and Severin Wirz.

Contents

Introduction

This is a book about *what* you should know about anti-bribery compliance, but it's worth spending a few minutes considering *why* this issue is important. The reasons go well beyond fear of prosecution. Prosecutorial priorities may well shift over time. Indeed, the current U.S. Administration is keen to emphasize its enthusiasm for rolling back regulations that make American companies less competitive.

The social arguments against bribery are compelling. Bribery of government officials constitutes theft from the public. Bribery undermines security when police, military, customs officials and border guards can be bought. Bribes are paid to ensure building inspectors look the other way, health officials approve unsafe products, toxic waste is disposed of inappropriately, and government contracts are awarded for inferior products at inflated prices.

But these arguments don't resonate with those who argue that corporations should focus on shareholder value and not on corporate social responsibility. Far too little is said in reply to explain how bad bribery is for business.

Well-run companies prefer predictability and bribery introduces uncertainty and delay. No contracts are signed formalizing bribes, so the negotiation never officially ends. Entrepreneurial bribe-takers identify or create opportunities for more demands. Delays increase as more people want in on the deal. The bribes themselves introduce delay: it takes time to generate the bribe funds, often through false invoices or non-existent subcontractors, and more time to bury the details in the company's books. And because bribery is illegal everywhere—whether or not the laws are actively enforced—there is no recourse when the bribe recipient reneges or sells the same deal to a higher bidder. Companies can't sue for breach of a bribe-tainted contract.

Companies suffer in other ways when management tolerates bribery. There is less enthusiasm for research and development when recourse to kickbacks ensures a sale. The sales team will spend less time differentiating and promoting products if the product matters less than the payoff. Talented employees will abandon companies where their contribution is marginalized by bribery schemes. On top of that, bad actors in international markets can be ostracized. Most people familiar with the international business community can name three or four of the worst offenders—so, at least anecdotally, this is already underway.

If the business argument against bribery is so strong, then, why does the U.S. government need to continue to lead the world in anti-bribery enforcement?

Bribery certainly accounts for some short-term successes. A mediocre sales team with a substandard product and inflated prices can still win the day with a well-placed bribe. Tolerating these market distortions is more costly to companies than developing a culture of compliance—U.S. companies lose more money to corrupt competitors than most ever spend on getting this issue right. Enforcement of anti-bribery laws against these companies helps preserve the benefits of market transparency.

The argument that U.S. enforcement puts American companies at a disadvantage isn't convincing. Its anti-bribery leadership role wins the United States supporters in challenging markets. U.S. companies are still lauded internationally for superior products. They're still considered to be prestigious partners in some measure because their reputation for good governance increases the perceived value of the undertaking. And, finally—for the cynics—anti-bribery enforcement added $2.48 billion to U.S. coffers in 2016 and only three of the ten companies that have been hit hardest by U.S. anti-bribery enforcement are headquartered in the United States.

The United States has led the world in addressing commercial bribery. G.W. Bush's administration emphasized the link between bribery and terrorism. Obama's administration underscored this argument and decried the human cost of bribery. If this Administration is to be as emphatically pro-business as we have been told, rolling back efforts to reduce bribery internationally would be a bad place to start.

For compliance professionals who understand the value of embracing transparency and deterring bribery regardless of shifting enforcement priorities, we hope you'll find this volume a useful resource.

Based on an article published by Alexandra Wrage in Forbes in January 2017.

Chapter 1
What You Should Know About Foreign Officials

The Foreign Corrupt Practices Act ("FCPA") prohibits the bribery of foreign government officials.[1] While the contours of the FCPA are complex and nuanced, few provisions have generated more confusion than the definition of "foreign official." Minimizing this confusion is critical for companies that do business in countries where the line between a "foreign official" and a private citizen is often quite murky. In this chapter, TRACE has created guidance to assist companies with this analysis so they can make informed decisions when conducting business abroad.

Who exactly qualifies as a foreign official for purposes of the FCPA? The statute's definition is deceptively simple:

> The term "foreign official" means any officer or employee of a foreign government or any department, agency, or instrumentality thereof, or of a public international organization, or any person acting in an official capacity for or on behalf of any such government or department, agency, or instrumentality, or for or on behalf of any such public international organization.[2]

---

[1] The FCPA also prohibits the bribery of foreign political parties or their officials, candidates for foreign political office, or "any person, while knowing that all or a portion of the payment will be offered, given, or promised to an individual falling within one of these three categories." *See* 15 U.S.C. § 78dd-1(a)(1)-(3), 78dd-2(a)(1)-(3), 78dd-3(a)(1)-(3). However, the FCPA makes clear that its prohibitions do not extend to the employees or agents of purely commercial entities. Moreover, payments to *foreign governments* as such are not prohibited, but the U.S. Department of Justice ("DOJ") has warned "companies contemplating contributions or donations to foreign governments ... [to] take steps to ensure that no monies are used for corrupt purposes, such as the personal benefit of individual foreign officials." A Resource Guide to the U.S. Foreign Corrupt Practices Act ("FCPA Guide") at 20, *available at* https://www.justice.gov/sites/default/files/criminal-fraud/legacy/2015/01/16/guide.pdf.

[2] 15 U.S.C. §§ 78dd-1(f)(1)(A), 78dd-2(h)(2)(A), 78dd-3(f)(2)(A).

Despite the simplicity of this definition, the U.S. government's interpretation of "foreign official" is quite broad. In many instances the analysis will be fairly straightforward. Identifying government departments and agencies, for example, is an uncomplicated task in most countries. And if an individual is an officer or employee of a foreign government department or agency,[3] he or she will undoubtedly qualify as a foreign official. However, under certain circumstances the analysis may be more challenging. Specifically, when does an entity qualify as an "instrumentality" of a foreign government? And when is a person acting "in an official capacity for or on behalf" of a foreign government department, agency or instrumentality?

When is an Organization an "Instrumentality" of a Foreign Government?

Few aspects of the FCPA have generated more attention (or litigation) than the definition of "instrumentality" of a foreign government. Similar to other provisions in the FCPA, the U.S. government has interpreted this term quite broadly, determining that an expansive range of organizations qualify under this standard. The most common application of this term has been to "state-owned enterprises" ("SOEs"), or "any corporate entity recognized by national law as an enterprise, and in which the state exercises ownership."[4] Companies may encounter SOEs in industries such as "aerospace and defense manufacturing, banking and finance, healthcare and life sciences, energy and extractive industries, telecommunications, and transportation."[5]

In some instances, an SOE's status as an instrumentality under the FCPA may be straightforward. However, when government ownership is not clear or the services provided by an entity do not appear inherently governmental in nature, companies may struggle to deter-

---

[3] Companies should also note the inclusion of "public international organizations" in the definition of "foreign official." This means that the prohibitions extend not only to the employees and officers of traditional government entities, but to the employees and officers of public international organizations as well (*e.g.*, the World Bank, Red Cross, International Monetary Fund, etc.)..

[4] OECD Guidelines on Corporate Governance of State-Owned Enterprises (2015), *available at* http://www.oecd.org/daf/ca/guidelines-corporate-governance-soes.htm.

[5] FCPA Guide at 20.

mine whether the entity falls within the purview of the FCPA. For instance, a common example of an SOE is found in China, where state-owned hospitals have become a compliance challenge for unwary companies that assume the entities are privately owned. Many companies have faced stiff fines and penalties from the U.S. government for gifts, hospitality and payments made to Chinese doctors, nurses, pharmacists, or hospital administrators to influence the purchase of goods and services. While the gifts and hospitality provided to these employees may be permissible in private hospitals, as employees of state-owned hospitals, such doctors, nurses, pharmacists, and hospital administrators are considered to be "foreign officials" under the FCPA.

In recent years, several companies have litigated the "instrumentality" issue, providing further guidance to companies that must undertake this challenging analysis. In the leading case, the U.S. Court of Appeals for the Eleventh Circuit affirmed the conviction of two individuals who had bribed officials of a Haitian telecommunications company.[6] The telecommunications company was the sole provider of landline telephone service in Haiti; it was 97% owned by the National Bank of Haiti (which is owned by the Haitian government); and the Haitian President appointed all of the company's board members.[7] It was not, however, designated as a government entity by law.[8] The defendants claimed that the telecommunications company was not an "instrumentality" of the Haitian government because it did not perform traditional, core government functions.[9] The Eleventh Circuit rejected the defendant's restricted interpretation of "instrumentality," preferring a fact-intensive approach to determining an entity's status.[10] Using the multi-factor approach outlined below, the court found that the telecommunications company was an "instrumentality" of the Haitian government and the officials were "foreign officials" under the FCPA.

The Eleventh Circuit defined an "instrumentality" as "an entity controlled by the government of a foreign country that performs a

---

[6] See *United States v. Esquenazi*, 752 F.3d 912 (11th Cir. 2014).

[7] *Id.* at 928–29.

[8] *Id.*

[9] *Id.* at 924.

[10] *Id.* at 925.

function the controlling government treats as its own."[11] The court outlined a non-exhaustive list of relevant factors that could help determine what constitutes "control" and what constitutes a "function the government treats as its own."[12]

To determine whether a government "controls" an entity, the following factors may be considered:

- The foreign government's formal designation of that entity;

- Whether the government has a majority interest in the entity;

- The government's ability to hire and fire the entity's principals;

- The extent to which the entity's profits, if any, go directly into the governmental fisc; and

- The extent to which the government funds the entity if it fails to break even[13].

To determine whether the entity performs a "function" that the government treats as its own, the following factors may be considered:

- Whether the entity has a monopoly over the function it exists to carry out;

- Whether the government subsidizes the costs associated with the entity providing services;

- Whether the entity provides services to the public at large in the foreign country; and

- Whether the public and the government of that foreign country generally perceive the entity to be performing a government function.[14]

---

[11] *Id.*

[12] *Id.* at 925–27.

[13] *Id.* at 925.

[14] *Id.* at 926.

Other cases have provided additional, non-exclusive factors that may be considered when making this determination,[15] including:

- The purposes of the entity's activities;

- The entity's obligations and privileges under the foreign country's laws;

- The circumstances surrounding the entity's creation;

- The level of financial support from the government (through, *e.g.*, subsidies, special tax treatment, loans, or financing from government-mandated taxes, licenses, fees or royalties).

While the Eleventh Circuit's guidance provides a framework for determining whether an entity constitutes an "instrumentality" under the FCPA, it necessitates a fact-intensive inquiry when encountering a new foreign entity. Thus any company seeking to determine whether it is dealing with an employee or official of an instrumentality must conduct an inquiry that enables it to address the factors outlined by the courts.

When is a Person Acting "in an Official Capacity for or on Behalf" of a Foreign Government Department, Agency or Instrumentality?

Once a company has determined that it is dealing with a government agency, department or instrumentality, an individual's status as a "foreign official" is generally a foregone conclusion. In certain instances, however, an individual's status or relationship to an entity may not be clear. Even if an individual is not an official or employee of an entity, he or she may still be working "for or on behalf" of a foreign government department, agency or instrumentality.

For example, a company may wish to retain a foreign consultant or agent with strong ties to the foreign government of a country in which the company plans to do business. Or a company seeking to expand business opportunities in a foreign country may be consid-

---

[15] *See, e.g.*, Criminal Minutes—Order Denying Motion To Dismiss Counts 1 through 10 of the Indictment, *United States v. Carson*, No. 09-cr-00077 (C.D. Cal. 18 May 2011); *United States v. Noriega*, No. 2:10-cr-01031 (C.D. Cal. 28 Feb. 2011).

ering doing business with a third party who has done or is currently doing work for the same government. In one FCPA enforcement action, a company settled FCPA allegations involving improper payments made to an "advisor to the Iranian Oil Minister" whose family controlled all oil and gas contract awards in Iran.[16] Although this individual was not employed by the Iranian government, given the influence he had with respect to government decisions, the U.S. government deemed him a "foreign official" under the FCPA.

Because the line between private citizen and foreign official can be murky, the DOJ has addressed the issue in written guidance to various companies.[17] For example, in 2010, a company sought DOJ guidance regarding its initiative with a foreign government.[18] The company planned to retain a consultant that had extensive contacts in the government of the foreign country, and that held contracts to represent the foreign government and act on its behalf. In its review of the proposed relationship, the DOJ noted that because the consultant was an agent of the foreign government, the consultant had acted and would continue to act on behalf of the foreign government—rendering the consultant and its employees "foreign officials" under the FCPA. However, in this instance, the company took affirmative steps to ensure that the consultant and its owner would not act on behalf of the foreign government under the proposed consulting agreement and would therefore not be considered foreign officials for purposes of the company inquiry. Specifically, the DOJ pointed to the consultant's "walling off" of employees working for the company from those continuing to work for the government; the full disclosure of the relationship to relevant parties; the permissibility of the relationships under local law; and contractual obligations to limit further representation of the foreign government by the consultant.[19]

---

[16] *In re Statoil, ASA*, SEC Administrative Proceeding File No. 3-12453 (13 Oct. 2006); DOJ Press Release No. 06-700, "U.S. Resolves Probe Against Oil Company That Bribed Iranian Official" (13 Oct. 2006).

[17] *See generally* FCPA Opinion Procedure Releases, *available at* https://www.justice.gov/criminal-fraud/opinion-procedure-releases.

[18] *See* FCPA Opinion Procedure Release 10-03 (1 Sept. 2010), *available at* https://www.justice.gov/sites/default/files/criminal-fraud/legacy/2010/09/01/1003.pdf.

[19] *Id.* at 4.

Although many companies may be nervous at the prospect of hiring a third party that has acted and continues to act on behalf of a foreign government, in its guidance the DOJ made it clear that payments to foreign officials are not always prohibited by the FCPA:

> [T]he FCPA does not per se prohibit business relationships with, or payments to, foreign officials. In such cases, the Department typically looks to determine whether there are any indicia of corrupt intent, whether the arrangement is transparent to the foreign government and the general public, whether the arrangement is in conformity with local law, and whether there are safeguards to prevent the foreign official from improperly using his or her position to steer business to or otherwise assist the company, for example through a policy of recusal.[20]

In 2012, the DOJ provided additional guidance regarding when an individual is acting on behalf of a foreign government. In this instance, a company sought guidance regarding its proposed contractual arrangement with a consulting company, one of whose partners belonged to the royal family of a foreign government.[21] Although the royal family member held no position in the government, the company wanted the DOJ's opinion regarding his status as a foreign official under the FCPA. While noting that it did not consider the partner a "foreign official" in this instance, the DOJ provided an outline of the factors companies should consider when determining the status of a royal family member under the FCPA.[22] The DOJ noted that "mere membership" in a royal family would not automatically qualify an individual as a foreign official, further explaining that this determination requires a "fact-intensive, case-by-case determination" of the following non-exhaustive list of factors:

- The structure and distribution of power within a country's government;

---

[20] *Id.* at 3.

[21] FCPA Opinion Procedure Release 12-01 (18 Sept. 2012), *available at* https://www.justice.gov/sites/default/files/criminal-fraud/legacy/2012/09/27/1201.pdf.

[22] *Id.* at 5.

- A royal family's current and historical legal status and powers;

- The individual's position within the royal family;

- An individual's present and past positions within the government;

- The mechanisms by which an individual could come to hold a position with governmental authority or responsibilities (such as, for example, royal succession);

- The likelihood that an individual would come to hold such a position; and

- An individual's ability, directly or indirectly, to affect governmental decision-making.

While the two preceding examples involve different scenarios, both make clear that the "foreign official" inquiry is a fact-intensive process that depends heavily on context. The DOJ has provided a useful framework for conducting this analysis, but it is up to companies to take affirmative steps to ensure they are in compliance with the FCPA.

Compliance Best Practices and Strategies

A company seeking to determine whether an individual is a foreign official under the FCPA should take the following steps before proceeding with an engagement or transaction:

1. **Due diligence.** All foreign-official determinations share a common theme: they are fact-intensive, context-heavy inquiries. Whether determining if an entity qualifies as an instrumentality of the state, or if an individual is acting on behalf of a foreign government, the process is the same. The company must gather all the facts necessary to address the multi-factored tests outlined by the DOJ and the courts. In addition, the company must document its due diligence process, including a written analysis demonstrating the steps it has taken to determine whether the individual qualifies as a foreign official under the FCPA.

2. **Contractual provisions.** Contractual provisions are a critical component of the compliance process. For example, to ensure that a third party will not be considered a "foreign official," a company may seek representations from the individual that he or she is not a foreign official, has no official role in the foreign government's decision-making processes that could influence business opportunities for the company, and is not working for or on behalf of the foreign government.

3. **"Walling-off" potential conflicts.** If a company intends to retain a third party that does work for or on behalf of a foreign government, extra precautions will be necessary. Specifically, the entity's employees who are performing work for or on behalf of the government must be walled-off from the employees working for the company. The "walling-off" process must be formalized in writing and employees must agree, in writing, that they will abide by these preventative measures.

4. **Obtain an opinion or letter.** When an entity's status as an SOE or an individual's relationship with a foreign government is in question, it is wise to obtain a local legal opinion to ensure these questions are answered. It may also be feasible to obtain a letter from the foreign government regarding the entity's status as an SOE or the government's relationship with a particular individual.

5. **Be transparent.** Although this step may not be necessary in every instance, the DOJ has expressed approval of arrangements under which the company has disclosed sensitive relationships to the foreign government. For example, when a company retained a consultant that frequently acted for or on behalf of a foreign government, the DOJ acknowledged that the company's disclosure of the relationship to the foreign government was a factor that influenced its approval of the arrangement.

6. **Train your employees.** It is critical that employees and third parties receive training regarding who qualifies as a foreign official under the FCPA. Although training employees is an important first step, in most instances it will be third parties (consultants, agents, brokers) interacting with the potential

foreign official. Because the "foreign official" analysis is so fact-intensive, it is critical that employees and third parties have more than a passing understanding of this issue. Consequently, robust training for third parties is necessary.

7. **Transaction monitoring, testing internal controls, and updating compliance procedures.** Given the risks associated with providing gifts, hospitality or even payments to potential foreign officials, companies should integrate the multi-factored "foreign official analyses" into their compliance programs. Because the risks may be heightened in certain countries and industries, transaction monitoring and the testing of internal controls and compliance procedures is also critical.

Companies should take note of the guidance provided by the courts and government and integrate the "foreign official analysis" into their compliance programs. This is particularly important for companies that do business with SOEs in high-risk jurisdictions. Because these multi-factored analyses can be complicated, companies should strongly consider handling them in consultation with legal counsel.

Chapter 2
What You Should Know About Items of Value

When people envision the bribery of a public official, they often imagine an individual handing a government official cash stuffed in a brown paper bag or suitcase. Although bribes may often take the form of cash, the universe of things that may constitute a bribe is incredibly broad and diverse.

To ensure that U.S. criminal law captures the full array of potential bribes, Congress has passed legislation that enables prosecutors to address corruption in its many different forms. In the international context, the FCPA achieves that goal by prohibiting the corrupt "offer, payment, promise to pay, or authorization of the payment of any money, or offer, gift, promise to give, or authorization of the giving of anything of value" to a foreign official.[1]

This chapter will answer the question: what is "anything of value" under the FCPA? Recent FCPA enforcement actions demonstrate that prosecutors have interpreted this phrase broadly—sometimes in surprising ways. This paper will provide readers with an overview of this aspect of the statute, as well as practical compliance tips.

"Anything of Value": An Overview

The FCPA prohibits, among other things, giving, promising to give, or authorizing the giving of "anything of value" to foreign government officials.[2] Although the statute does not define "anything of value," judicial interpretations of this phrase may be found in domestic corruption cases.[3] The phrase has been interpreted by courts as

---

[1] 15 U.S.C. §§ 78dd-1(a); 78dd-2(a); 78dd-3(a) (emphasis added).

[2] *Id.*

[3] *See* A Resource Guide to the U.S. Foreign Corrupt Practices Act ("FCPA Guide"), at 108 n.86, *available at* https://www.justice. gov/sites/default/files/criminal-fraud/legacy/2015/01/16/guide.pdf.

encompassing a wide array of tangible and intangible items, including "things" that may be difficult to value, such as conjugal visits,[4] the testimony of a witness,[5] and information.[6] Moreover, the phrase "has been broadly construed to focus on the worth attached to the bribe by the defendant, rather than its commercial value."[7]

The FCPA does not contain a minimum threshold for what constitutes a thing of value, though the government has acknowledged that "it is difficult to envision any scenario in which the provision of cups of coffee, taxi fare, or company promotional items of nominal value" would be prosecuted.[8] The government has made clear, however, that it will prosecute (and has prosecuted) cases in which there has been a pattern of giving small gifts and payments to a foreign official that evidences a "scheme to corruptly pay foreign officials to obtain or retain business."[9]

To be prosecuted, the person or company giving the thing of value must have "corrupt intent"—the intent to improperly influence a foreign government official.[10] The government has explained the significance of corrupt intent in determining whether a gift or payment violates the Act: "The corrupt intent requirement protects companies that engage in the ordinary and legitimate promotion of their businesses while targeting conduct that seeks to improperly induce officials into misusing their positions."[11]

Corrupt intent may be demonstrated not only when the gift or payment is given directly to a foreign official, but also when it is given through intermediaries or to interested third parties. The government views this as an indirect attempt to influence a foreign government official—and therefore prosecutable under the FCPA. For

---

[4] *See United States v. Marmolejo*, 89 F.3d 1185 (5th Cir. 1996).

[5] *See United States v. Zouras*, 497 F.2d 1115 (7th Cir. 1974).

[6] *See United States v. Sheker*, 618 F.2d 607 (9th Cir. 1980).

[7] U.S. Department of Justice Criminal Resource Manual § 2044, *available at* https://www.justice.gov/usam/criminal-resource-manual-2044-particular-elements (citing *United States v. Williams*, 704 F.2d 603, 622–23 (2d Cir.), cert. denied, 464 U.S. 1007 (1983)).

[8] FCPA Guide at 15.

[9] *Id.*

[10] *Id.*

[11] *Id.*

example, in *United States v. Liebo*, the vice president of a large aerospace firm bought plane tickets for the honeymoon of a family member of a government official from Niger.[12] Liebo's company sought contracts with the Ministry of Defense and the tickets were given to the cousin of a government official who could (and eventually did) influence the contract award. Liebo was "sentenced to 18 months in prison, suspended with three years' probation, with 60 days of home confinement and 600 hours of community service."[13]

Similarly, in 2010, Alcatel-Lucent S.A. and three of its subsidiaries paid USD 137 million to settle an FCPA enforcement action for bribery of officials in Costa Rica, Honduras, Malaysia, and Taiwan.[14] The company retained consultants in those countries to pass bribes along to government officials who were in a position to award business to the company. Although the company never paid the foreign officials directly, they were still liable under the FCPA for these indirect payments, funneled through intermediaries.

"Anything of Value" in Practice

Although many recent FCPA enforcement actions have been based on the transfer of cash or cash-equivalents to foreign officials, numerous other FCPA enforcement actions involve the giving of gifts, hospitality, travel and entertainment. Although the government has been clear that "a small gift or token of esteem or gratitude is often an appropriate way for business people to display respect for each other," large or extravagant gifts to foreign officials have triggered enforcement actions.[15]

U.S. officials have also noted that "widespread gifts of smaller items" may be prosecuted if perceived to be part of a pattern of bribes.[16] Despite abundant warnings from the government regarding this issue,

---

[12] *United States v. Liebo*, 923 F.2d 1308 (8th Cir. 1991).

[13] Richard L. Cassin, "May it Please the Court" (1 May 2008), *available at* http://www.fcpablog.com/blog/2008/5/2/may-it-please-the-court.html.

[14] DOJ Press Release No. 10-1481, "Alcatel-Lucent S.A. and Three Subsidiaries Agree to Pay $92 Million to Resolve Foreign Corrupt Practices Act Investigation" (27 Dec. 2010), *available at* https://www.justice.gov/opa/pr/alcatel-lucent-sa-and-three-subsidiaries-agree-pay-92-million-resolve-foreign-corrupt.

[15] FCPA Guide at 15.

[16] *Id.*

companies continue to run afoul of the FCPA through the provision of gifts and hospitality to foreign government officials.

For example, in 2009, UTStarcom Inc. settled an FCPA enforcement action based on the gifts, hospitality and travel it provided to employees of state-owned telecommunications firms in China in an attempt to secure telecommunications contracts.[17] The company arranged for the employees to visit "popular tourist destinations in the United States, including Hawaii, Las Vegas and New York City."[18] Similarly, in an effort to win a contract from a government-run telecommunications entity in Thailand, the company spent nearly USD 10,000 on French wine and USD 13,000 on entertainment as a gift to agents of the government customer. UTStarcom paid USD 3 million to settle its FCPA enforcement action with the DOJ and SEC.

In 2015, FLIR Systems Inc. settled an FCPA enforcement action based on the gifts and hospitality it provided to Saudi government officials who played a "key role" in decisions to award it business.[19] According to the SEC, the company "provided expensive watches to government officials of the Saudi Arabia Ministry of Interior in 2009, and they arranged for the company to pay for a 20-night excursion by Saudi officials that included stops in Casablanca, Paris, Dubai, Beirut, and New York City." In addition, the company paid for several "New Year's Eve trips to Dubai with airfare, hotel, and expensive dinners and drinks." FLIR agreed to pay USD 9,504,584 to settle the FCPA enforcement action.

Although providing gifts, hospitality, and travel to foreign officials has been a source of significant liability for many companies, the U.S. government recognizes that certain expenditures are necessary to pursue legitimate business opportunities. Because companies frequently need to meet with foreign officials to perform contract requirements, conduct training, or provide demonstrations, the FCPA includes an affirmative defense designed to provide comfort and

---

[17] DOJ Press Release No. 09-1390, "UTStarcom Inc. Agrees To Pay $1.5 Million Penalty for Acts of Foreign Bribery in China" (31 Dec. 2009), *available at* https://www.justice.gov/opa/pr/utstarcom-inc-agrees-pay-15-million-penalty-acts-foreign-bribery-china.

[18] *Id.*

[19] SEC Press Release No. 2015-62, "SEC Charges Oregon-Based Defense Contractor With FCPA Violations" (8 Apr. 2015), *available at* https://www.sec.gov/news/pressrelease/2015-62.html.

guidance to companies who must pay for these types of expenses in order to conduct business.

This affirmative defense precludes liability under the FCPA for "reasonable and bona fide" expenditures incurred by or on behalf of a foreign official "directly related" to the promotion, demonstration or explanation of products or services or the execution or performance of a contract with a foreign government or agency.[20] This defense permits companies to pay "reasonable and bona fide" expenses, so long as they are directly related to the promotion or demonstration of a product or the performance of a government contract.

The affirmative defense is broadly worded and provides companies with flexibility to pay necessary expenses in order to conduct business with foreign governments. It is not, however, a free pass to provide foreign officials with gifts and hospitality in an effort to improperly obtain or retain business. Over the past decade, there have been numerous instances of companies crossing the line from "reasonable and bona fide" expenditures to bribes.

For example, in 2007, Lucent Technologies, Inc. settled an FCPA enforcement action for the extensive gifts and hospitality it provided to Chinese government officials.[21] The company spent over USD 10 million sponsoring trips to sightseeing locations such as Disneyland, Universal Studios, Niagara Falls and the Grand Canyon, and cities such as Los Angeles, San Francisco, Las Vegas, Washington, D.C. and New York. The company also provided between USD 500 and 1,000 per day to the traveling foreign officials as a "per diem." The trips were often characterized in the company's books and records as "factory inspections" or "training" pursuant to contracts with the Chinese government, even though the trips were mostly unrelated to the company's business. Despite the company's attempt to shoehorn the hospitality and travel into the FCPA's affirmative defense, the government rejected the characterization, finding that the conduct violated the FCPA. Lucent agreed to pay USD 2.5 million in fines and penalties to settle the enforcement action.

---

[20] 15 U.S.C. §§ 78dd-1(c), 78dd-2(c), 78dd-3(c).

[21] *SEC v. Lucent Technologies. Inc.*, Civil Action No. 1:07-cv-02301 (D.D.C. filed 21 Dec. 2007); DOJ Press Release No. 07-1028, "Lucent Technologies Inc. Agrees To Pay $1 Million Fine To Resolve FCPA Allegation" (21 Dec. 2007).

Similarly, Aon Corporation settled an FCPA enforcement action in 2011 with the DOJ and SEC for improper travel and hospitality expenditures paid on behalf of foreign officials in an attempt to obtain and retain insurance business.[22] Although the company designated funds to pay for foreign officials' attendance at insurance seminars and conferences, it spent the money on non–training related activities, such as travel, hotels, meals, entertainment, and "extensive" leisure activities in tourist destinations including London, Paris, Monte Carlo, Zurich, Munich, Cologne and Cairo. In some instances, the company covered expenditures for family members of the government officials as well. The trips had little to do with business and lacked a connection to the insurance industry. The company settled the enforcement action by paying USD 16.2 million in fines and penalties.

The DOJ has provided guidance to help companies comply with the FCPA and ensure that their conduct falls within the perimeters of the affirmative defense. Specifically, the government has made it clear that expenditures "will not give rise to prosecution if they are (1) reasonable, (2) bona fide, and (3) directly related to (4) the promotion, demonstration, or explanation of products or services or the execution or performance of a contract."[23]

Because the determination regarding whether an expenditure is "reasonable" or "bona fide" is necessarily fact-specific, the government has provided a "non-exhaustive" list of guidelines that a company may consult before making such expenditures:[24]

- Do not select the particular officials who will participate in the party's proposed trip or program or else select them based on pre-determined, merit-based criteria;

- Pay all costs directly to travel and lodging vendors and/or reimburse costs only upon presentation of a receipt;

- Do not advance funds or pay for reimbursements in cash;

---

[22] *SEC v. Aon Corp.*, Civil Action No. 1:11-cv-02256 (D.D.C. filed 20 Dec. 2011).

[23] FCPA Guide at 24.

[24] *Id.*

- Ensure that any stipends are reasonable approximations of costs likely to be incurred and/or that expenses are limited to those that are necessary and reasonable;

- Ensure the expenditures are transparent, both within the company and to the foreign government;

- Do not condition payment of expenses on any action by the foreign official;

- Obtain written confirmation that payment of the expenses is not contrary to local law;

- Provide no additional compensation, stipends, or spending money beyond what is necessary to pay for actual expenses incurred;

- Ensure that costs and expenses on behalf of the foreign officials will be accurately recorded in the company's books and records.

The government has expressly noted that the FCPA "does not prohibit gift-giving."[25] It does, however, prohibit bribes disguised as gifts. To ensure compliance with the FCPA, the government has recommended that companies have "clear and easily accessible guidelines and processes in place for gift-giving by the company's directors, officers, employees, and agents" in order to control gift-giving, deter improper gifts and hospitality, and protect corporate assets.[26]

Recent Developments

In recent years, the breadth of the government's interpretation of the phrase "anything of value" has been highlighted in several FCPA enforcement actions and investigations. It has been particularly notable in cases involving charitable donations and the hiring of foreign officials' relatives.

For example, in 2007, the pharmaceutical company Schering-Plough settled an enforcement action with the SEC. In an effort to persuade

---

[25] *Id.* at 16.

[26] *Id.*

a Polish foreign official to purchase the company's pharmaceutical products, the company's Polish subsidiary made charitable donations to a foundation dedicated to the restoration of castles.[27] Although the charity was legitimate, the government found that the company made the donations in an attempt to improperly influence the foreign official. The government pointed to the fact that the foreign government official was the head of the foundation. Moreover, the donations were inconsistent with the company's pattern of charitable giving (it was the only organization to receive multiple donations from the company) and constituted a significant portion of the company's promotional budget. The company also concealed the nature of the payments in the company's books and records by disguising them as medical expenditures. The company paid USD 500,000 to settle the case.

In 2016, Nu Skin settled an FCPA enforcement action with the SEC for its "charitable contributions."[28] The company's Chinese subsidiary made a payment of RMB 1 million (approximately USD 154,000) to a charity in exchange for a Chinese official's intervention in a government investigation of the company. Specifically, the company's Chinese subsidiary was under investigation for failure to comply with local laws and had been threatened by the government with the imposition of a fine of RMB 2.8 million (approximately USD 431,000). The Chinese subsidiary offered to donate money to a charity identified by a high-ranking Chinese official in exchange for his intervention in the matter. The Chinese subsidiary notified its U.S. parent about the donation, but failed to disclose the connection between the charity and the investigation. It also removed anti-corruption language from the final donation agreement, despite guidance from outside counsel. Within days of the donation ceremony, the Chinese subsidiary learned that the government would not charge or fine the company.[29] The company paid USD 776,000 to settle the enforcement action.

---

[27] *SEC v. Schering-Plough Corp.*, Civil Action No. 1:04CV00945 (D.D.C. filed 8 June 2004), *available at* https://www.sec.gov/litigation/complaints/comp18740.pdf.

[28] Securities Exchange Act of 1934 Release No. 78884 and Administrative Proceeding File No. 3-17556 (21 Sept. 2016), *In the Matter of Nu Skin Enterprises, Inc.*, *available at* https://www.sec.gov/litigation/admin/2016/34-78884.pdf.

[29] In addition to the charitable donation, the company also agreed to expedite college recommendation letters for the official's child.

Although charitable donations pose a risk under the FCPA, the government has been clear that not all charitable donations will result in liability under the statute. To assist companies seeking to make charitable donations, the government has provided guidance to companies to help ensure their compliance with the FCPA.[30] The DOJ has approved proposed donations or grants when companies have implemented the following due diligence measures and controls:

- Certifications by the recipient regarding compliance with the FCPA;

- Due diligence to confirm that none of the recipient's officers were affiliated with the foreign government at issue;

- A requirement that the recipient provide audited financial statements;

- A written agreement with the recipient restricting the use of funds;

- Steps to ensure that the funds were transferred to a valid bank account;

- Confirmation that the charity's commitments were met before funds were disbursed;

- On-going monitoring of the efficacy of the program.

As the government has noted: "Legitimate charitable giving does not violate the FCPA. Compliance with the FCPA merely requires that charitable giving not be used as a vehicle to conceal payments made to corruptly influence foreign officials."[31]

In recent years, companies have also run afoul of the FCPA by employing family members of foreign government officials in order to obtain and retain business. The government views these jobs and internships to be "things of value" under the FCPA. For example, in 2015, BNY Mellon settled an FCPA enforcement action brought because it had provided internships to the family members of two

---

[30] FCPA Guide at 19.

[31] *Id.*

officials of a Middle Eastern sovereign wealth fund.[32] The family members—a son and nephew of one official and the son of a second official—received the internships without meeting the hiring criteria for the positions. Although the interns were allegedly unqualified for the positions, internal emails demonstrated that company employees viewed the internships as necessary to maintain business dealings with the sovereign wealth fund. Among other things, the SEC found that the company "failed to devise and maintain" a system of internal controls regarding its hiring practices "sufficient to provide reasonable assurances that its employees were not bribing foreign officials in contravention of company policy." The company paid USD 14.8 million to settle the case with the SEC.

In 2016, Qualcomm Incorporated also settled an FCPA enforcement action based on the hiring of relatives of Chinese government officials responsible for deciding whether to buy the company's mobile technology products.[33] The company allegedly referred to these hires (for jobs and paid internships) as "must place" or "special" hires given their relationship to influential Chinese officials. The company also provided a USD 75,000 research grant to a U.S. university on behalf of a foreign official's son so he could retain his position in a Ph.D. program and renew his student visa. The company also gave him an internship and later permanent employment despite his initial interview which resulted in a "no hire" decision because he lacked the skills and failed to comply with minimum hiring criteria. Indeed, company interviewers noted that "he would be a drain on teams he would join." In addition, a company executive personally provided the official's son with a USD 70,000 loan to buy a home. In settling the case, Qualcomm agreed to pay a USD 7.5 million penalty and to self-report to the SEC for the next two years with annual reports and certifications of its FCPA compliance.

---

[32] SEC Press Release No. 2015-70, "SEC Charges BNY Mellon With FCPA Violations" (18 Aug. 2015), *available at* https://www.sec.gov/news/pressrelease/2015-170.html; *In the Matter of The Bank of New York Mellon Corp.*, Admin. Pro. File No. 3-16762 (2015), *available at* https://www.sec.gov/litigation/admin/2015/34-75720.pdf.

[33] *In the Matter of Qualcomm Inc.*, Admin. Pro. File No. 3-17145 (2016), *available at* https://www.sec.gov/ litigation/admin/2016/34-77261.pdf. (The company also "provided frequent meals, gifts, and entertainment with no valid business purpose to foreign officials to try to influence their decisions, such as airplane tickets for their children, event tickets and sightseeing for their spouses, and luxury goods.")

The "charitable donation" and "hiring" cases demonstrate the government's broad interpretation of the phrase "anything of value"—especially with regard to intangible items. Similar to gifts and hospitality, the government recommends that companies integrate policies and procedures into their compliance programs to address these particular risks.

Compliance Tips

As the U.S. government continues to interpret the phrase "anything of value" quite broadly, companies face an increasing risk of liability under the FCPA. To reduce this risk, companies should develop and implement robust compliance policies and procedures that address this rapidly developing area of enforcement. The following compliance tips will help companies to mitigate or even prevent potential FCPA violations:

- Companies must keep in mind that the universe of potential bribes is virtually limitless. The government interprets the phrase "anything of value" broadly and the FCPA does not impose a minimum dollar threshold on gifts or payments. Thus the universe of "things of value" that may constitute bribes is vast, and companies must be aware of the risks associated with the provision of "things of value" to government officials. Companies must train employees to recognize traditional and non-traditional forms of bribery.

- This is not the commercial sector. Many FCPA cases involve gifts and hospitality expenditures that may be legal to exchange in a private sector setting. Any "thing of value" could be viewed as a bribe if perceived to be valuable by the recipient and given in an attempt to improperly influence a foreign government official.

- Reduce your risk. Companies may reduce the risk of potential FCPA liability by implementing robust, risk-based compliance policies and procedures. This must include comprehensive gift and hospitality and charitable donation policies as well. Companies should require employees—particularly those that interact with foreign officials—to undergo routine training to ensure they understand the expansive nature of the FCPA. Companies must also ensure that they actually follow their anti-corruption policies and procedures, as the government has treated the failure to do so harshly in recent FCPA enforcement actions.

- Gift and hospitality best practices. Companies should ensure that their compliance policies and procedures reflect industry best practices with regard to gifts and hospitality. The policies should be regularly reviewed and updated to ensure they capture the lessons learned from recent enforcement actions. Companies should also implement robust tracking and accounting procedures to ensure all gifts and hospitality are monitored and documented. TRACE's Gifts, Travel & Hospitality Tracking Software enables companies to easily monitor, track and report on employee expenditures and reinforce company policies with automated compliance reminders.

- Stay within the contours of the "promotional" defense. Although the FCPA's allowance for reasonable and bona fide promotional expenditures is quite generous, companies must monitor any expenditures that may fall within the perimeters of this affirmative defense to ensure compliance with the statute. Indeed, companies should prohibit the payment of promotional expenses (*i.e.*, travel, hospitality, entertainment) on behalf of foreign officials without the written approval of the company's compliance department. Compliance professionals must ensure that any requested expenditures of this nature are reasonable and serve a legitimate business purpose.

- Is that donation truly charitable? Companies should develop and implement robust policies and procedures regarding charitable donations. Donations must be reasonable, appropriate, lawful, consistent with the company's policies and procedures, given openly and transparently, provided without the expectation of the award or retention of business, and accurately documented in the company's books and records. Any requests to make a charitable donation should, among other things, address the purpose of the donation and the relationship (if any) to foreign officials who may be in a position to award business to the company. Companies must conduct thorough and well-documented due diligence before making charitable donations to verify potential connections to foreign officials. Companies should also continue to monitor the charitable organization's use of a donation to ensure that it is being used properly and for its intended purpose.

- Ensuring FCPA compliance when making hiring decisions. FCPA compliance programs should address potential human-resource risks to ensure that practices comply with the FCPA. All HR policies and procedures should be followed during a hiring process; any deviations from hiring criteria should be justifiable, documented, and transparent. Company procedures should flag candidates that may create FCPA risks. Any candidates with a relationship to a foreign official must follow company hiring procedures, meet company hiring criteria, apply (and be hired) without involvement of the foreign official, and be reviewed by internal compliance professionals to ensure compliance with the FCPA. Companies should provide training to HR employees (or other personnel involved in the hiring process) to ensure they understand potential FCPA risks and are well-acquainted with internal hiring procedures and standards.

Companies must stay abreast of developments in global anti-corruption enforcement to ensure their policies and procedures address new areas of risk and industry best practices. There are numerous resources available to companies seeking concise and informative updates, including the TRACE Compendium and the TRACE Matrix. TRACE also publishes Gifts & Hospitality Guidelines for almost every country which highlight legal and cultural issues raised when gifts and meals are provided to foreign government officials.

Chapter 3
What You Should Know About International Due Diligence Standards

In designing and implementing an anti-bribery compliance program, your top priority is to minimize the likelihood of bribes being paid or offered to public officials on your company's behalf. That on its own is a sufficiently worthy goal—we all understand the financial, societal, and personal harm that accompanies institutional corruption. At the same time, companies need to be attentive to the expectations of regulators, legislators, and the public. Bribery is a serious offense, both criminal and civil, and can bring significant penalties and enormous reputational damage to those who engage in it. To avoid or minimize that damage, one must be duly diligent in ascertaining the background and monitoring the behavior of those who carry out the company's business.

But what qualifies as adequate due diligence? How do you incorporate due diligence into your company's compliance program in a manner that will not only reduce the chance of bribery as far as possible, but also satisfy the enforcement authorities if, notwithstanding your efforts, a problem does arise?

All circumstances are unique, of course, and each company's compliance program needs to be tailored to its own situation. There are nevertheless a number of authoritative sources for guidance on how such programs should be structured and what degree of due diligence they should include. These range from national enforcement agencies, like the **Department of Justice** and **Securities and Exchange Commission** in the U.S. and the **Ministry of Justice** and **Serious Fraud Office** in the UK, to intergovernmental entities like the **Organisation for Economic Co-operation and Development**, the **United Nations**, and the **World Bank** that have either promulgated anti-corruption conventions or adopted anti-corruption standards for their lending programs, as well as trade and advocacy organizations like the **International Chamber of Commerce** and **Transparency International**.

The guidance provided by these organizations generally follows a unified direction, representing a broad consensus on the appropriate nature and measure of anti-bribery due diligence. Each institution's guidance nevertheless has its own history, context, and concerns. Rather than attempting to distill this guidance into a single set of directives, the aim of this chapter is to review the various authorities, identify the documents in which their guidance is set forth, and provide a brief analysis of the principles articulated therein. We hope this will help you navigate your way through the body of official due-diligence standards as you work to build or maintain a compliance program appropriately suited to your company's needs.

National Enforcement Agencies

The most important guidance regarding anti-bribery due diligence standards arguably comes from the government agencies that enforce a given country's anti-bribery laws. They are the ones who decide which allegations to investigate and which companies or individuals to charge with violations, and they have substantial leeway in settlement discussions to scale the penalty to the severity of the offense. This latter calculation often involves consideration of an offending company's compliance program, including whether the due diligence conducted by the company is deemed to have been adequate. It is therefore critical to know what those enforcement agencies consider to be adequate due diligence.

Here, we will focus on the agencies that enforce the two most prominent national laws governing transnational bribery: the FCPA and the UK Bribery Act 2010.

U.S. Department of Justice / U.S. Securities and Exchange Commission

The DOJ and the SEC are jointly responsible for enforcing the FCPA. The FCPA was enacted in 1977 following discovery of the widespread use of "slush funds" by American companies to pay bribes overseas, and was subject to significant amendments in 1988 and

1998. The law broadly prohibits the payment of bribes to foreign officials, mandates the implementation of adequate controls to prevent such practices, and requires that accounting records be accurately maintained. The DOJ enforces the FCPA criminally against both companies and individuals, and civilly against "domestic concerns"; the SEC has civil-enforcement authority over U.S.–listed public companies and those who act on their behalf.

Both agencies maintain collections of online FCPA-related resources at their respective websites.[1] The most comprehensive of these is a 120-page guidebook published jointly by the two agencies in November 2012 entitled "A Resource Guide to the U.S. Foreign Corrupt Practices Act" (the "FCPA Resource Guide").[2] The Guide notes that it is "non-binding, informal, and summary in nature," and should not be relied on as a substitute for competent legal advice. At the same time, it contains the best single summary available of the agencies' expectations regarding corporate compliance programs.[3]

Specifically, Chapter 5 of the FCPA Resource Guide ("Guiding Principles of Enforcement")[4] discusses at length the factors considered by the DOJ and the SEC in deciding whether to open investigations or bring charges against a company, based on the principles set forth in their respective enforcement manuals.[5] Those factors

---

[1] *See* "Foreign Corrupt Practices Act" (DOJ), *available at* http://www.justice.gov/criminal/fraud/fcpa; "Spotlight on Foreign Corrupt Practices Act" (SEC), *available at* http://www.sec.gov/spotlight/fcpa.shtml.

[2] *Available at* https://www.justice.gov/criminal-fraud/fcpa-guidance.

[3] After the original publication of this white paper, the DOJ published an eight-page guidance document on "Evaluation of Corporate Compliance Programs" (8 Feb. 2017), offering a condensed summary of "some important topics and sample questions that the Fraud Section has frequently found relevant in evaluating a corporate compliance program." With respect to third-party due diligence, the guidance addresses the topics of Risk-Based and Integrated Processes, Appropriate Controls, Management of Relationships, and Real Actions and Consequences. The document is available at https://www.justice.gov/criminal-fraud/page/file/937501/download.

[4] FCPA Resource Guide at 52.

[5] *See* Principles of Federal Prosecution of Business Organizations, U.S. Attorney's Manual § 9 28.000 et seq. (DOJ 1997, rev. Nov. 2015), *available at* https://www.justice.gov/usam/usam-9-28000-principles-federal-prosecution-business-organizations; Enforcement Manual (SEC 4 June 2015), *available at* http://www.sec.gov/divisions/enforce/enforcementmanual.pdf.
    It should also be noted that the DOJ's enforcement decisions are necessarily informed by certain provisions of the U.S. Sentencing Guidelines ("USSG") governing corporate culpability and conditions of probation—specifically USSG § 8B2.1, "Effective

include "the existence and effectiveness of the corporation's pre-existing compliance program," with the elements of such a program addressed in greater depth under the headings "Corporate Compliance Program," "Hallmarks of Effective Compliance Programs," and "Other Guidance on Compliance and International Best Practices."[6]

The fundamental message these sections convey is that one size doesn't fit all. "Effective compliance programs are tailored to the company's specific business and to the risks associated with that business. They are dynamic and evolve as the business and the markets change."[7] The agencies make it clear there is no single set of elements that must be included or procedures that must be followed:

> DOJ and SEC have no formulaic requirements regarding compliance programs. Rather, they employ a common-sense and pragmatic approach to evaluating compliance programs, making inquiries related to three basic questions:
>
> • Is the company's compliance program well designed?
>
> • Is it being applied in good faith?
>
> • Does it work?[8]

The agencies actively discourage mechanical implementation of their suggestions: "Compliance programs that employ a 'check-the-box' approach may be inefficient and, more importantly, ineffective. Because each compliance program should be tailored to an organization's specific needs, risks, and challenges, the information provided below should not be considered a substitute for a company's own assessment of the corporate compliance program most appropriate for that particular business organization."[9]

Compliance and Ethics Program." *See* FCPA Resource Guide at 56. Those provisions include the requirement that organizations "exercise due diligence to prevent and detect criminal conduct," USSG § 8B2.1(a)(1) (rev. 1 Nov. 2015), which may include "monitoring and auditing to detect criminal conduct," USSG § 8B2.1(b)(5)(A), but they do not otherwise specify standards or protocol for performing due diligence on third-party intermediaries.

[6] FCPA Resource Guide at 56.

[7] *Id.* at 56.

[8] *Id.*

[9] *Id.* at 57.

The elements of an effective program as described by the agencies will be familiar to compliance professionals: "Commitment from Senior Management and a Clearly Articulated Policy Against Corruption"; "Code of Conduct and Compliance Policies and Procedures"; "Oversight, Autonomy, and Resources"; "Risk Assessment"; "Training and Continuing Advice"; "Incentives and Disciplinary Measures"; "Confidential Reporting and Internal Investigation"; and "Continuous Improvement: Periodic Testing and Review."

Most relevant for the present analysis, however, is the agencies' advice regarding "Third-Party Due Diligence and Payments." Observing that "third parties, including agents, consultants, and distributors, are commonly used to conceal the payment of bribes to foreign officials in international business transactions," the agencies set forth three major guiding principles for conducting due diligence on such intermediaries:

1. Obtain and understand critical information about intermediaries, including their qualifications, associations, business reputation, and relationships with foreign officials;

2. Understand why and how the intermediary is being used: the business rationale, the contract and payment terms, whether those terms are typical under the circumstances, and whether the work is performed as directed;

3. Periodically review relationships with third-party intermediaries, including updated due diligence, audits, ongoing training, and regular compliance certification.[10]

The agencies emphasize that a company's due diligence on its intermediaries should be "risk-based," and that "the degree of appropriate due diligence may vary based on industry, country, size and nature of the transaction, and historical relationship with the third party."[11]

---

[10] *See id.* at 60.

[11] *Id.*

Finally, the Guide identifies resources from other U.S. government agencies[12] and a range of international organizations[13] addressing the elements of an effective compliance program. These resources are presented as exemplars of "an emerging international consensus on compliance best practices."[14] We will examine several of these resources more closely below, fleshing out the contours of this consensus.

UK Ministry of Justice

On 8 April 2010, following decades of debate and consideration, the UK Parliament updated and consolidated its century-old anti-bribery laws by enacting the UK Bribery Act 2010 ("UKBA"). The UKBA—which became effective on 1 July 2011—criminalizes both "active" bribery (offering, promising, or paying a bribe) and "passive" bribery (requesting, assenting to, or accepting a bribe). It specifically prohibits bribery of foreign public officials for business advantage, and imposes liability on corporations that fail to prevent bribery undertaken on their behalf. Unlike the FCPA, the UKBA does not include any provision regarding the accurate maintenance of financial records.

Notably, the UKBA includes an explicit defense against corporate liability for failing to prevent bribery. As set forth in Section 7(2), "it is a defense for [a commercial organisation] to prove that [the organisation] had in place adequate procedures designed to prevent persons associated with [the organisation] from undertaking such conduct." Anticipating the need for further information on what constitute "adequate procedures," Section 9(1) of the UKBA directs the Secretary of State to "publish guidance about procedures that relevant commercial organisations can put in place to prevent persons associated with them from bribing."

---

[12] *See id.* at 63 (citing U.S. Dept. of Commerce, Business Ethics: A Manual for Managing a Responsible Business Enterprise in Emerging Market Economies (2004), *available at* http://www.ita.doc.gov/goodgovernance/adobe/bem_manual.pdf, and U.S. Dept. of State, Fighting Global Corruption: Business Risk Management (2d ed. 2001), *available at* http://www.ogc.doc.gov/pdfs/Fighting_Global_Corruption.pdf).

[13] *See id.* (citing publications by the Organisation for Economic Co-operation and Development; the Asia-Pacific Economic Cooperation; the International Chamber of Commerce; Transparency International; the United Nations Global Compact; the World Bank; and the World Economic Forum).

[14] *Id.*

Pursuant to that mandate, in March 2011 the Secretary of State for Justice published his formal **Guidance about procedures which relevant commercial organisations can put into place to prevent persons associated with them from bribing (section 9 of the Bribery Act 2010)** ("UKBA Guidance" or the "Guidance"),[15] along with a more informal "quick start guide."[16] Both documents describe "the six principles" that should inform a company's anti-bribery procedures: (1) Proportionality; (2) Top Level Commitment; (3) Risk Assessment; (4) Due Diligence; (5) Communication; (6) Monitoring and Review. The Guidance emphasizes that the six principles are not intended to be prescriptive, but "flexible and outcome focussed, allowing for the huge variety of circumstances that commercial organisations find themselves in."[17] In particular, consistent with the first principle, "bribery prevention procedures should be proportionate to risk."[18]

The Guidance articulates the fourth principle, "Due Diligence," as follows:

> The commercial organisation applies due diligence procedures, taking a proportionate and risk based approach, in respect of persons who perform or will perform services for or on behalf of the organisation, in order to mitigate identified bribery risks.[19]

Bribery risks will vary (as explained in connection with the third principle) depending on the country in which business is being conducted or sought, the sector in which the company operates, the nature of the transaction, the value and complexity of the business opportunity, and the party with whom one is dealing.[20] The Guidance anticipates that due diligence will be used as a tool both for assessing risk in a given circumstance, and for mitigating the risk indicated by such an assessment.

---

[15] *Available at* https://www.justice.gov.uk/downloads/legislation/bribery-act-2010-guidance.pdf.

[16] *Available at* https://www.justice.gov.uk/downloads/legislation/bribery-act-2010-quick-start-guide.pdf.

[17] UKBA Guidance at 20.

[18] *Id.*

[19] *Id.* at 27.

[20] *Id.* at 26.

Beyond reinforcing that due diligence should be "proportionate" and "risk-based," the Guidance recommends certain steps that might be appropriate in higher-risk situations, including direct inquiries, indirect investigations, and "general research on proposed associated persons."[21] Such steps may be taken from within the company or by external consultants,[22] and may focus on company employees occupying high-risk positions as well as on third-party intermediaries.

As an appendix, the Guidance includes a series of illustrative hypothetical case studies—complementing but not part of the official guidance provided in the body of the document. The studies "should not be seen as standard setting, establishing any presumption, reflecting a minimum baseline of action or being appropriate for all organisations whatever their size."[23] This reflects the Guidance's overall emphasis on general principles and its reluctance to impose specific requirements on companies, whether regarding due diligence or other aspects of their compliance programs. As the Secretary indicated in the Guidance's forward, for the Ministry of Justice, "combating the risks of bribery is largely about common sense, not burdensome procedures."[24]

Intergovernmental Entities

While national enforcement agencies have a certain discretion in determining what level of due diligence will spare a company the punitive consequences of an act of bribery, it is ultimately the countries' legislatures that set the rules and confer that discretion. Intergovernmental entities play a crucial role in encouraging national governments to adopt laws prohibiting bribery, and they wield significant oversight authority when the terms of such laws have been agreed to by convention.

Both the OECD and the United Nations have adopted conventions requiring signatory nations to take certain anti-corruption measures, including passing anti-corruption laws. Although these organizations do not have the power to enforce such laws directly, they

---

[21] *Id.* at 28.

[22] *Id.* at 27.

[23] *Id.* at 32.

[24] *Id.* at 2.

remain significant sources of authority regarding how that enforcement should take place. We will therefore examine what they have to say about adequate anti-bribery due diligence. We will also look briefly at the due-diligence standards articulated by another inter-governmental organization, the World Bank, that has a vested interest in ensuring its funds are not used for corrupt purposes.

The Organisation for Economic Co-operation and Development

Founded in 1960, the OECD is an organization of 35 member states whose mission is "to promote policies that will improve the economic and social well-being of people around the world."[25] In late 1997, the OECD adopted its Convention on Combating Bribery of Foreign Public Officials in International Business Transactions (the "OECD Convention"),[26] which became effective in February 1999. The OECD Convention requires adopting states (all 35 current member countries, plus six additional signatories) to criminalize the bribery of foreign public officials. The OECD monitors and periodically conducts formal peer review of participants' implementation efforts. The ratification of the OECD Convention was the primary basis for the 1998 amendments to the FCPA by the United States, and the organization's review efforts were a significant motivating force behind the United Kingdom's passage of the UKBA.

In late 2009, the OECD significantly updated its anti-bribery framework by issuing a Recommendation of the Council for Further Combating Bribery of Foreign Public Officials in International Business (the "2009 Recommendation"). [27] Among other things, the 2009 Recommendation called on Convention signatories to ensure that companies are liable for bribery undertaken for their benefit by agents and intermediaries.[28] The OECD Council also adopted its "Good Practice Guidance on Internal Controls, Ethics, and

---

[25] http://www.oecd.org/about/.

[26] *Available at* http://www.oecd.org/daf/anti-bribery/ConvCombatBribery_ENG.pdf.

[27] *Available at* http://www.oecd.org/daf/anti-bribery/44176910.pdf.

[28] *See* "About the 2009 Recommendation for Further Combating Bribery of Foreign Public Officials in International Business," *available at* http://www.oecd.org/daf/anti-bribery/2009_Anti-Bribery_Recommendation_Brief.pdf.

Compliance" (the "OECD Guidance")[29] —a short set of non-legally-binding guidelines to help companies comply with the new recommendations.

The principles set forth in the OECD Guidance are presented as "flexible" and "intended to be adapted by companies ... according to their individual circumstances, including their size, type, legal structure and geographical and industrial sector of operation, as well as the jurisdictional and other basic legal principles under which they operate."[30] Many of these principles are familiar from other sources of guidance: strong commitment by senior management; a clear and visible anti-bribery policy; independent internal monitoring; adequate financial controls; appropriate educational measures, incentives, and disciplinary procedures; protection for whistleblowers; and periodic program review. With respect to due diligence, the OECD Guidance is both straightforward and open-ended: compliance programs should include "properly documented risk-based due diligence pertaining to the hiring, as well as the appropriate and regular oversight of business partners."[31]

The United Nations

The OECD Convention (like the FCPA) is relatively focused in scope: prohibiting transnational bribery of government officials, with penalties for those who pay bribes or on whose behalf bribes are paid. It does not impose liability on those who solicit or accept bribes.

Shortly after the OECD Convention went into effect, the United Nations undertook a more all-encompassing endeavor. In October 2003, it adopted the United Nations Convention Against Corruption ("UNCAC"),[32] negotiated under the auspices of the U.N. Office on Drugs and Crime. The UNODC's website describes the UNCAC (which became effective on 14 December 2005) as taking a "far-reaching approach" to develop "a comprehensive response to a global problem."[33] In addition to bribery, "[t]he UNCAC covers

---

[29] *Available at* https://www.oecd.org/daf/anti-bribery/44884389.pdf.

[30] *Id.* at Introduction.

[31] *Id.* at § A.6.i.

[32] *Available at* https://www.unodc.org/unodc/en/treaties/CAC/.

[33] https://www.unodc.org/unodc/en/corruption/index.html.

many different forms of corruption, such as trading in influence, abuse of power, and various acts of corruption in the private sector."[34] The UNCAC has been ratified or otherwise adopted by a total of 178 countries.[35]

The UNCAC is lengthy and wide-ranging, with a total of 71 articles. Among these, Article 16 is our point of comparison. Entitled "Bribery of foreign public officials and officials of public international organizations," Article 16 requires each adopting state to criminalize the intentional promising, offering, or giving to a public official of an "undue advantage" (money presumably qualifying) in order to obtain business "or other undue advantage" in the conduct of international business. The inverse scenario is also addressed, but with reservation: the Article invites adopting states to "consider" criminalizing the public official's solicitation or acceptance of an "undue advantage," but does not require such legislation.

Given the range of the UNCAC's concerns, it is not surprising to find an abundance of available guide materials. Among the more relevant for the private-sector is **An Anti-Corruption Ethics and Compliance Program for Business: A Practical Guide**,[36] which includes an extended discussion on "[a]pplication of the anti-corruption programme to business partners," such as agents and intermediaries.[37] Specific due-diligence recommendations are prefaced with the familiar caveat that "[t]he scope and intensity of due diligence for selecting partners may be determined by the company's overall risk assessment," factoring in considerations such as industry, country, scope of work, and prior familiarity, among others.[38] With that in mind, the guide suggests a variety of possible inquiries:

- Checks on legal status and type of organization of the business partner, including jurisdiction of incorporation;

---

[34] *Id.*

[35] *See* https://www.unodc.org/unodc/en/treaties/CAC/signatories.html.

[36] U.N. Office on Drugs and Crime (Sept. 2013), *available at* https://www.unodc.org/documents/corruption/Publications/2013/13-84498_Ebook.pdf.

[37] *See id.* at 54–62.

[38] *See id.* at 58.

- Assessment of the financial or organizational dependencies and ownership structures of the business partner (*e.g.* company partly owned by the government);

- Determination of any conflict of interests of key personnel from the business partner;

- Assessment of anti-corruption commitment from senior management of the business partner (*e.g.* active participation in voluntary anti-corruption initiatives);

- Accumulation of reputational information on the business partner (*e.g.* through consultations with other partners, local business associations, embassies);

- Review of corruption-related track record (*e.g.* past incidents, debarment cases); and

- Evaluation of the quality of the existing anti-corruption programme of the business partner.[39]

Such inquiries should facilitate the identification of red flags and help the company assess the risks of further engagement and possible means of risk-mitigation. "In cases where the company is not able to obtain sufficient information or cannot encourage the potential business partner to engage in risk mitigating activities, the company should not engage with this partner and should seek alternatives."[40]

Also of note is the semi-affiliated United Nations Global Compact,[41] "a voluntary initiative based on CEO commitments to implement universal sustainability principles and to take steps to support UN goals."[42] The Compact is organized around ten Principles, the last of which is that "[b]usinesses should work against corruption in all its forms, including extortion and bribery."[43] In furtherance of this Principle, the Compact has published several guides containing

---

[39] *Id.*

[40] *Id.*

[41] *See* https://www.unglobalcompact.org/.

[42] https://www.unglobalcompact.org/about.

[43] https://www.unglobalcompact.org/what-is-gc/mission/principles/principle-10.

useful discussions of compliance programs, including the conducting of due diligence.[44]

The World Bank

A year and a quarter into his tenure as President of the World Bank—and more than a year before the OECD Convention went into effect—James Wolfensohn used the occasion of the Bank's 1996 Annual Meetings to promote a "new development compact" that, he argued, would better address the needs of both donor and borrower countries. The new model would emphasize transparency and accountability in Bank projects, recognizing corruption as a "cancer" that stifles development and drives away private investment.[45]

Fighting corruption has remained a priority for the Bank. One way it pursues this aim is by maintaining "a zero-tolerance policy toward corruption in its projects."[46] In October 2006, it formalized that policy by issuing its "Guidelines On Preventing and Combating Fraud and Corruption in Projects Financed by IBRD Loans and IDA Credits and Grants."[47] In short, all recipients of Bank funds "must take all appropriate measures to prevent and combat fraud and corruption, and refrain from engaging in, fraud and corruption in connection with the use of the proceeds of IBRD or IDA financing."[48] Those who fail to do so are subject to sanctions, primarily debarment from further participation in Bank projects.[49]

---

[44] *See, e.g.*, Fighting Corruption in the Supply Chain: A Guide for Customers and Suppliers (U.N. Global Compact, June 2010), *available at* https://www.unglobalcompact.org/docs/issues_doc/Anti-Corruption/Fighting_Corruption_Supply_Chain.pdf; Business Against Corruption: Case stories and examples (U.N. Global Compact, Apr. 2006), *available at* https://www.unglobalcompact.org/docs/issues_doc/7.7/BACbookFINAL.pdf.

[45] *See* World Bank Archivists' Chronology: 1944–2013, at 310, *available at* http://www.worldbank.org/en/about/archives/history/chronology

[46] http://www.worldbank.org/en/topic/governance/brief/anti-corruption.

[47] *Available at* http://siteresources.worldbank.org/INTLEGSTAFONLY/Resources/AnticorruptionGuidelinesOct2006RevisedJan2011.pdf (revised Jan. 2001).

[48] Abstract, *available at* http://documents.worldbank.org/curated/en/551241468161367060/Guidelines-on-preventing-and-combating-fraud-and-corruption-in-projects-financed-by-IBRD-loans-and-IDA-credits-and-grants.

[49] *See* "Debarment with Conditional Release & Integrity Compliance / Summary of World Bank Group Integrity Compliance Guidelines," *available at* http://siteresources.worldbank.org/INTDOII/Resources/Integrity_Compliance_Guidelines.pdf.

In order for a sanctioned party to end its debarment, it must at a minimum implement or reinforce an integrity compliance program. As a framework for such rehabilitation, the Bank has published a short **Summary of World Bank Group Integrity Compliance Guidelines**,[50] incorporating "standards, principles and components commonly recognized by many institutions and entities as good governance and anti-fraud and corruption practices."[51] As is typical for such guidelines, they were issued with the caveat that "[t]hey are not intended to be all-inclusive, exclusive or prescriptive; rather a party's adoption of these Guidelines, or variants thereof, should be determined based on that party's own circumstances."[52]

The Guidelines contain a number of familiar compliance-program elements, such as clear prohibition of misconduct, a strong anti-corruption leadership stance, initial and periodic risk assessment and review, and adequate internal controls. They also contain specific direction regarding the performance of due diligence—both on employees and on business partners. The company should "[v]et current and future employees with any decision-making authority or in a position to influence business results, including management a Board members, to determine if they have engaged in Misconduct or other conduct inconsistent with an effective Integrity Compliance Program."[53] With respect to business partners (including agents, advisors, consultants, and other third parties), the company should do the following:

> Conduct properly documented, risk-based due diligence (including to identify any beneficial owners or other beneficiaries not on record) before entering into a relationship with a business partner, and on an on-going basis. Avoid dealing with contractors, suppliers and other business partners known or (except in extraordinary circumstances and where appropriate mitigating actions are put in place) reasonably suspected to be engaging in Misconduct.[54]

---

[50] *See id.*

[51] *Id.*

[52] *Id.*

[53] *Id.* at § 4.1.

[54] *Id.* at § 5.1.

In addition to promoting and enforcing its own policies, the World Bank has collaborated with the OECD and the U.N. Office on Drugs and Crime to produce a very useful overview document: the **Anti-Corruption Ethics and Compliance Handbook for Business,** published in 2013.[55] The collaboration had its origin in the observation that "the myriad of existing anti-corruption principles for business can be confusing, especially for small and medium-sized enterprises with limited resources."[56] There was no intention "to create new standards or represent any form of legally binding requirements for businesses," but only "to serve as a useful, practical tool for companies seeking compliance advice in one, easy-to-reference publication."[57] It is a good place to turn to better understand the context and content of the wide range of available anti-corruption guidance.

Trade and Advocacy Organizations

Although they have no enforcement authority with respect to anti-bribery or other anti-corruption law, trade and advocacy organizations have an interest in promoting standards of good and effective behavior in these areas. We will briefly discuss the contributions of two such organizations.

The International Chamber of Commerce

Founded in 1919, the International Chamber of Commerce was an early leader in promoting anti-bribery standards for businesses. In 1977—the same year the FCPA was enacted—the ICC issued the first version of its "Rules of Conduct to combat Extortion and Bribery." The document, now entitled the **ICC Rules on Combating Corruption** (2011),[58] addresses the full range of compliance-related concerns, including discussion of appropriate policies and the elements of an efficient compliance program.

---

[55] *Available at* https://www.unodc.org/documents/corruption/Publications/2013/Anti-CorruptionEthicsComplianceHandbook.pdf.

[56] *Id.* at 3.

[57] *Id.*

[58] *Available at* http://www.iccwbo.org/Data/Policies/2011/ICC-Rules-on-Combating-Corruption-2011/.

With respect to business partners (including third-party agents and intermediaries), the ICC Rules emphasize the principle of clear and explicit communication of the company's ethical commitments and expectations, the contractual memorialization of those expectations, and the maintenance of complete records of the business relationship—including names, terms of engagement, and payments made.[59] It is recommended that the company undertake "appropriate due diligence" with respect to the reputation of its business partners and their ability, when exposed to corruption risks, "to comply with anti-corruption law in their dealings with or on behalf of the Enterprise."[60] Along with the other ICC Rules, these principles are presented principally as "good commercial practice," to be applied in a manner conforming to controlling legal instruments.

Transparency International

Since 1993, the non-profit non-governmental organization Transparency International has promoted a broad anti-corruption agenda through its work with governments, businesses, and civil institutions. Its major contribution to the fight against bribery has been the publication of the **Business Principles for Countering Bribery**,[61] originally in 2002, with later editions released in 2009 and 2013. The most recent edition has been complemented by publication of the **Business Principles for Countering Bribery Commentary**.[62] Aspiring to the status of "an authoritative business anti-bribery code,"[63] the Business Principles includes a familiar range of compliance-program suggestions. The principles regarding business relationships (Section 6.2) include implementing a compliance program in each entity over which a company has effective control; encouraging other businesses in which the company has a "significant investment" or with which it has "significant business relationships" to adopt their own equivalent programs; conducting due diligence in connection with any merger, acquisition, or significant investment, as well as before appointing

---

[59] *See id.* at 7.

[60] *Id.*

[61] *Available at* http://www.transparency.org/whatwedo/tools/business_principles_for_countering_bribery.

[62] *Available at* http://www.transparency.org/files/content/publication/2015_BusinessPrinciplesCommentary_EN.pdf.

[63] *Id.* at 2.

agents, lobbyists, or other intermediaries; avoiding doing business with known or reasonably-suspected bribe-payers; reasonable and proportionate monitoring of significant business relationships; and preparing adequate compliance-related documentation.

Practical Application of Due-Diligence Principles

A recurring theme in the authorities we have discussed is that due diligence should be carried out in a "risk-based" and "proportionate" manner. That is, the extent and form of due diligence should be tailored with respect to the bribery risks involved in the particular industry, country, and project at issue, as well as the individuals and entities being reviewed.

What does that mean in practice? Experienced compliance professionals will be familiar with a range of information that can be obtained about a given subject, at varying levels of scrutiny and intrusiveness. The challenge is to know which inquiries are appropriate for each set of circumstances your company faces.

To meet that challenge, is can be helpful to consider not only what information might be sought, but for what *purpose*. In this final section, we aim to understand how the concrete elements of due diligence are related to and informed by the principles articulated by the leading authorities. In doing so, we hope to encourage and assist in the thoughtful and reasoned implementation of due-diligence programs.

General Principles of Due Diligence: A Short Review

To summarize, here are the specific suggestions we have seen from the leading national and intergovernmental authorities:

U.S. DOJ / SEC	• Obtain relevant basic information about your intermediaries.
	• Understand what they do for you and why you are using their services.
	• Review your intermediary relationships periodically.

UK Ministry of Justice	• Information can be obtained in various ways: by direct inquiry, through indirect investigation, or by means of general research on the proposed associations. • Due diligence activities may appropriately be conducted by external consultants. • In addition to intermediaries and other third-party associations, a company may wish to conduct due diligence on its employees in high-risk situations.
OECD	• An effective ethics and compliance program should include, as an essential element, "properly documented risk-based due diligence pertaining to the hiring, as well as the appropriate and regular oversight of business partners."
United Nations	• Where and how is the subject entity organized? Who owns it? Is it financially or organizationally entwined with any other entities? • Do any key personnel present conflicts of interest? Has senior management demonstrated a commitment to anti-corruption? • What is the subject's business reputation? Does it have a good corruption-related track record? How robust is its anti-corruption program?
World Bank	• Companies should perform due diligence on current and future employees, officers, and directors who have significant influence or decision-making authority. • Due diligence of business partners should include identification of beneficial owners and other beneficiaries. • Avoid dealing with contractors, suppliers, and others whom you reasonably suspect of engaging in misconduct.

Specific Elements of Due Diligence: An Overview

A due-diligence program can and should be informed by the principles and suggestions articulated by these authorities—including, above all, the principle that the level and scope of due diligence ought to be proportionate to the bribery risks in a given situation.

At the same time, it can be helpful to have a baseline from which proportions can be drawn. Certain information is always needed about a potential intermediary or business partner, if only for the sake of determining what other kinds of information might be called for. We will here sketch out some of the principal categories, drawing upon the collective experience of the compliance community in the years since the first modern anti-bribery laws went into effect. The overall relevance or importance of a given item may change over time, depending in part on the priorities of enforcement agencies and their case-by-case determinations regarding the adequacy of particular due-diligence implementations. *The following is accordingly not intended, and should not be taken, as legal advice regarding the appropriateness of any specific element or set of elements for a particular due-diligence program or situation.*

Background Information

Any due diligence inquiry begins with the company's or individual's basic identifying information: **full legal name**, any **aliases or trade names**, physical and mailing addresses, telephone numbers, and any **website** information. You will also want to have the name, telephone number, and email address of an appropriate **contact person** within the company.

In order to perform any significant research on the company, you will need its basic registration information, including the **date and place of establishment/incorporation**, any **tax identification numbers**, and copies of registration documents. If the entity has subsidiaries or other affiliates or is involved in any **joint ventures**, you should obtain information about those entities as well.

Your due diligence should include an understanding of the reason you are engaging this person or company—what your aims are, and how the engagement will contribute to those aims. You will therefore want information about the **primary industry** or industries in which the subject entity operates and the **services** it offers. Because each place in the world carries a different set of corruption risks, it can be helpful to know in what **countries or regions** the entity conducts business, and therefore what kinds of conditions they are likely to be familiar with and prepared for.

Ownership and Personnel

To the greatest extent possible, you want to ensure that anyone you engage will be acting in your best interests, without conflict or ulterior motive. You therefore need to know **who owns and controls the company**. If the company is wholly or partially owned by another corporate entity, you will need to know that entity's ownership information as well—all the way up to the individual **true beneficial owners**. With that information, you can better ascertain whether the company has any governmental ties or other connections that could signal a greater risk of corrupt behavior.

For the same reason, you may also need to obtain information about the **financial interests and relevant connections of key personnel** in the company, including its officers and directors. You should also have an understanding of the company's own financial interests, and whether any of them could present a conflict of interest. An **audited financial statement** might be requested accordingly.

Capacity to Perform Work Legitimately

An audited statement can also help you evaluate the entity's financial health. A company that is under financial pressure is considered more likely to give in to the temptations of corruption than a company whose finances are fundamentally strong. In addition, a healthy company may be better able to carry out its assignment through legitimate means, and not be tempted to take dangerous shortcuts. **Financial references** can also help with this assessment.

Evaluating a company's ability to do its work legitimately is a crucial element of due diligence. If you are engaging the company to perform a task requiring technical expertise, you should consider it a serious red flag if nobody at the company has the relevant training and experience. Under such circumstances, you should require the company to provide you with **CVs for the personnel** who will be involved in your project. **Professional references** are another way to evaluate whether a company is prepared for the job. Certain projects may also require substantial time and resources, which you want to make sure the company you engage can provide—for example, by knowing **the company's size** as well as any **other commitments** that might drain its capacity.

Compliance Standards and Commitment

Corruption isn't usually something a company sets out to engage in, but it is something a company can take positive steps to keep from happening. It is important not only that your own company has an ethical culture and effective compliance procedures; you want the companies you work with, or that work on your behalf, to be similarly vigilant. You should find out whether the company has a **code of ethics** or **anti-corruption policy**, and should request a copy of the same. Depending on the circumstances, it may also be appropriate to conduct a **compliance audit** to ensure that the company has adequate procedures in place to detect and prevent bribery and other corruption, and that senior management has demonstrated a strong adherence to anti-corruption principles. If the company has any history of noncompliance, that will be a strong warning to proceed carefully with the engagement, or simply call it off.

Conclusion

We have reviewed a range of leading sources of guidance regarding the construction and implementation of anti-bribery compliance programs, with particular attention to articulated standards of adequate due diligence of business agents and intermediaries. We have seen both that there is general agreement about the elements that should go into designing a due-diligence program, and at the same time that those elements are typically presented as guidelines, to be flexibly adapted to the needs, risks, and circumstances faced by each individual organization.

Above all, due diligence requires careful judgment. It is about understanding your business situation, the people and organizations you're dealing with, and the risks involved in the anticipated transactions. The most important thing is to ensure that you have sufficient information to evaluate the risks, to make informed decisions, and to follow through with appropriate ongoing monitoring. There is a broad consensus among the leading authorities that adequate due diligence is not achieved by mechanical implementation of a given set of procedures, but by the thoughtful evaluation and coordination of a broad set of possible inquiries, to be deployed in a reasoned and principled fashion. We hope this chapter has given you a helpful tour of the major authoritative sources for such principles and techniques.

Chapter 4
What You Should Know
About Accounting Provisions

When drafted in 1977, the FCPA's internal accounting provision was designed to increase public confidence in securities markets by requiring corporations to make assurances that their record-keeping was honest. Despite this desire for greater clarity, the internal controls provision of the FCPA remains among the most misunderstood and contentious areas of U.S. anti-bribery law. In this chapter, we address some of the common misconceptions and challenges that persist in our understanding of this provision, and explain what companies are doing to respond to those challenges.

The language of the provision, found in section 13(b)(2)(B) of the Securities Exchange Act,[1] is short and deceptively straightforward. Companies that are regulated by the SEC are required to devise and maintain a system of internal accounting controls. Those controls must provide "reasonable assurances" that the company's management is properly overseeing authorization for transactions and access to assets, and that the company's financial statements are in conformity with generally accepted accounting principles (GAAP).

Over the past four decades, the SEC has used the internal controls provision of the FCPA as a crucial instrument in regulating issuers' bookkeeping. Of the 22 cases brought by the SEC under the FCPA in 2016, all 22 included charges under section 13(b)(2)(B). This reflects the overall trend in the agency's enforcement history—in fact, of the 88 FCPA cases brought by the SEC since 2010, all but one have involved charges pursuant to the internal controls provision.

Despite the provision's frequent use, its application remains controversial. Questions surrounding the SEC's application of section 13(b)(2)(B) include whether violations of the internal controls provision

---

[1] *Codified at* 15 U.S.C. § 78m.

must entail actual corruption, as the FCPA's name implies; whether mere control failures—in the absence of any actual harm—violate the FCPA; and to what standard a company's accounting controls are to be held under the provision. To understand these concerns, we have conducted a holistic review of the cases brought under the internal controls provision, revisiting the assumptions underlying the SEC's application of the statute in light of the FCPA's legislative history. Our aim is to provide clarity, where we can, for companies seeking to comply with the FCPA and to shine a light on those issues that require more guidance from the SEC to better clarify the law's requirements.

Section 13(b)(2)(B) of the Securities Exchange Act of 1934

§ 13. Periodical and Other Reports

(b)(2) Every issuer which has a class of securities registered pursuant to section 12 of this title and every issuer which is required to file reports pursuant to section 15(d) of this title shall—

. . .

(B) devise and maintain a system of internal accounting controls sufficient to provide reasonable assurances that—

(i) transactions are executed in accordance with management's general or specific authorization;

(ii) transactions are recorded as necessary (I) to permit preparation of financial statements in conformity with generally accepted accounting principles or any other criteria applicable to such statements, and (II) to maintain accountability for assets;

(iii) access to assets is permitted only in accordance with management's general or specific authorization; and

(iv) the recorded accountability for assets is compared with the existing assets at reasonable intervals and appropriate action is taken with respect to any differences.

Covered Activity Under the Internal Controls Provision

For a company to be found guilty under the internal accounting controls provision, must the SEC show the occurrence of some underlying wrongful activity? In typical cases, a company's internal controls violation naturally stems from some attendant bribery activity involving a foreign government official. The criminal charge and the civil charge go hand-in-hand: one punishes the improper act, the other punishes the company's weak system of internal controls that allowed the act to occur in the first place.

Take, for example, the USD 45 million settlement between the SEC and Alcatel Lucent in 2010. The SEC alleged that the company made millions of dollars in payments through its subsidiaries to government officials throughout the world. According to the SEC's complaint, the company's subsidiaries falsified books and records, entered into agreements retroactively, used false invoices and payment documentation under business consulting agreements, and allowed manual cash disbursements without documentation, among other things.[2] In Alcatel's case, the internal controls violation was fairly straightforward: had the company's compliance and accounting teams put in place an adequate control system, the bribes could have been detected earlier and maybe even prevented altogether.

More controversial among the FCPA bar is the SEC's increasing activity against companies under the internal controls provision even where no actual bribe has occurred. Much of the commentary has surrounded the 2012 case brought against Oracle Corporation, in which Oracle's Indian subsidiary used its local distributors to help set aside more than USD 2.2 million of sales proceeds into non-company accounts. Notably, there was no evidence that the set-aside money was actually used to pay bribes—though the SEC's complaint did allege that the parked funds "potentially could be used for illicit means, such as bribery or embezzlement."[3]

---

[2] *See* TRACE Compendium – Alcatel Lucent, *available at* http://traceinternational.org/compendium.

[3] *SEC v. Oracle Corp.*, CV 12 4310 CRB (N.D. Cal.), Litigation Release No. 22450 (16 Aug. 2012).

SEC v. Oracle Corp.

The SEC filed a complaint against Oracle Corporation in the U.S. District Court for the Northern District of California on 16 August 2012. The SEC complaint alleged that between 2005 and 2007, employees of Oracle India Private Limited ("Oracle India"), Oracle's Indian subsidiary, had distributors for the company set aside a portion of their sales proceeds—derived from an undisclosed mark-up on sales to the Indian government—so that the funds wouldn't appear in the company's records. Over a dozen transactions were allegedly structured in this way, with a total of USD 2.2 million set aside. Oracle India employees would then allegedly instruct the distributors to use the set-aside funds to pay third parties, some of which were not on Oracle's approved vendor list, and some of which did not even exist as legitimate businesses.

Oracle discovered irregularities in India while conducting routine audits of its Asia division. Once the problem of the "parked funds" was discovered, the company conducted additional due diligence on its partner transactions in India, terminated its relationship with the suspect distributor, and instructed other distributors not to allow funds to be set aside. Oracle also enhanced its anti-corruption training programs.

The senior Channel Sales Manager for Oracle India resigned in November 2007. Following an audit by Oracle's Asia Division, four other Oracle India employees were dismissed for allowing or actively participating in the scheme.

Commentators have attacked the reasoning in Oracle, saying that it presents "a very dangerous slippery slope,"[4] offers "a stunning result"[5] and effectively turns the FCPA into "a strict liability statute."[6] "The government can rely on the Oracle precedent as a backstop for every investigation—if the government cannot prove bribery then they need only show that there is a 'risk' of bribery," writes FCPA commentator Michael Volkov. "The case sets a dangerous precedent and a real stretch of the FCPA statute."[7]

However, the SEC has consistently viewed the purview of the FCPA as broader than corruption, and even the potential for corruption. The history of how the accounting provision came to be included within the FCPA is instructive here. In the early 1970s, before passage of the FCPA, there was an initiative within the accounting industry to standardize accounting controls to ensure public confidence in the ways in which financial information was being reported. At the time, publicly-traded companies were using various accounting methods that made it more difficult for investors to rely on financial statements. With the support of the SEC, the Financial Accounting Standards Board (FASB) was established in 1973, and shortly thereafter the FASB began publishing standards to be observed in the presentation of audited accounts and financial statements. A year later, the SEC began investigating a large number of bribery scandals revealing how off-the-books accounts were being used to funnel bribes to foreign government officials.

When Congress invited the SEC to suggest language for inclusion in early versions of FCPA, the Commission sought to use the Act as a mechanism for furthering ideals of assuring corporate accountability which, up until that time, had been attempted primarily through voluntary cooperation. As Lloyd Feller, former counsel at the SEC

---

[4] Michael Volkov, "A Closer Look at Internal Controls Enforcement" (10 Apr. 2015), *available at* http://www.law360.com/articles/641956/a-closer-look-at-internal-controls-enforcement.

[5] William J. Stuckwisch & Matthew J. Alexander, "The FCPA's Internal Controls Provision: Is Oracle an Oracle for the Future of SEC Enforcement?", Criminal Justice Magazine, Vol. 28, No. 3 (Fall 2013).

[6] Mike Koehler, "The Dilution Of FCPA Enforcement Has Reached A New Level With The SEC's Enforcement Action Against Oracle" (17 Aug. 2012), *available at* http://fcpaprofessor.com/the-dilution-of-fcpa-en- forcement-has-reached-a-new-level-with-the-secs-enforcement-action-against-oracle/.

[7] *See* "A Closer Look at Internal Controls Enforcement," *supra* note 4.

and now a partner at the law firm of Morgan & Lewis wrote in 1982, "the [FCPA], as it is applied through the accounting provisions, has absolutely nothing to do with foreign corrupt practices; it has to with accounting, including the maintenance of books and records, and the establishment and maintenance of a system of internal accounting controls."[8] Establishing a base level for corporate accounting controls was therefore seen as an important prerequisite for confidence in financial reporting.[9]

As a result, many of the SEC's early cases under the internal accounting provisions of the FCPA had nothing to do with foreign bribery.[10] Instead, they were primarily intended to penalize companies that failed to put in place the most basic accounting controls. In one early case involving a wholesale dealer of rare coins, the company was found guilty under section 13(b)(2)(B) for having failed to safeguard its physical inventory, maintain adequate purchase orders, require employees to keep receipts, or generally maintain adequate documentation to support the keeping of reasonably accurate books and records.

> The establishment and maintenance of a system of internal controls is an important management obligation. A fundamental aspect of management's stewardship responsibility is to provide shareholders with reasonable assurances that the business is adequately controlled. Additionally, management has a responsibility to furnish shareholders and potential investors with reliable financial information on a timely basis. An adequate system of internal accounting controls is necessary to management's discharge of these obligations.
>
> – Senate Report No. 95-114 (1977)

Far from being an outlier, as some have suggested,[11] *Oracle* conforms to this longstanding tradition within the SEC of using the FCPA

---

[8] Lloyd Feller, "An Examination of the Accounting Provisions of the FCPA," 9 Syracuse J. Int'l L. & Com. 245 (1982).

[9] *See e.g.*, *SEC v. Crown Cork & Seal Co., Inc.*, Civ. Act No. 81-2065, (D.D.C.), Litigation Release No. 9437 (2 September 1981); *SEC v. El Dorado International, Inc.*, Civ. Act No. 81.0532 (D.D.C.), Litigation Release No. 9314 (5 March 1981).

[10] *SEC v. World-Wide Coin Investments*, 567 F. Supp. 724, 751 (N.D. Ga. 1983).

[11] *See e.g.*, Paul Weiss Client Memorandum, "SEC Extends Application of FCPA Accounting Provisions in BHP Billiton Enforcement Action" (28 May 2015), *available at* https://

to set a standard for corporate accounting systems. Slush funds, like the one Oracle's Indian subsidiary put in place, fall squarely within the type of accounting failures that the provision was intended to prevent. *Oracle* also serves as a reminder of the broad reach of the internal control requirements under the FCPA. The provision operates similarly to a strict liability requirement insofar as any issuer subject to regulation by the SEC is expected to provide reasonable assurances that its system of internal accounting controls is working. That the issuer conducts business abroad or even with foreign government officials is ultimately irrelevant.

Establishing "Reasonable Assurances" Under the Act

To what standard are a company's accounting controls to be held under section 13(b)(2)(B)? While the SEC must show that a company's internal controls system is inadequate, there are no specific standards by which to evaluate the sufficiency of those controls. The Act simply states that a company's system of internal accounting controls must provide "reasonable assurances" that transactions are recorded accurately. What qualifies as "reasonable" is left open to interpretation.

Again, the history behind the statute is instructive here. As designed, section 13(b)(2)(B) was intended to ensure that companies put controls in place that would safeguard the accuracy of their financial statements. By including the internal accounting controls provision in the FCPA, the SEC wished to supplement those efforts by the FASB to standardize the way in which public companies were already beginning to put accounting controls in place. In drafting the provision, Congress borrowed directly from the accounting literature and intentionally referenced generally accepted accounting principles (GAAP) in the statute so that people would interpret the language in the same way that accountants had already been doing for years.[12] Far from establishing any new requirements or expectations for

---

www.paulweiss.com/media/2946569/28may15alert.pdf.

[12] *See* "An Examination of the Accounting Provisions of the FCPA," 9 Syracuse J. Int'l L. & Com. 245 (1982).

companies, the provision largely sought to bring companies more into conformity with one another.

Many in the FCPA community have been alarmed, therefore, by the SEC's increasingly aggressive and prescriptive approach in this area. In 2012, the SEC and the DOJ published a joint guide to the FCPA which stated that "[a]n effective compliance program is a critical component of an issuer's internal controls."[13] In the same document, the two agencies listed ten "Hallmarks of an Effective Compliance Program," touching on such areas as training, third party due diligence, and disciplinary measures. This policy position presents a significant departure from the statute's original language, which discusses "accounting controls" in terms more closely tied to effective bookkeeping. GAAP, for example, does not impose any requirements for employee anti-bribery training or third party due diligence.

The SEC's case-record shows its willingness to enforce compliance measures under section 13(b)(2)(B).[14] Unsurprisingly, many have viewed the SEC's application of the internal controls provision as a misapplication of the statute. William Stuckwisch, former DOJ prosecutor and now a partner at Kirkland & Ellis, writes that the SEC's application of the internal accounting controls "conflates the provision's requirements for sufficient 'internal accounting controls' with the continually evolving elements of an 'effective' compliance program."[15] This conflation has only led to more confusion under the statute, reinforcing the misconception that the internal controls provision of the FCPA is primarily aimed at curbing foreign corruption—something the SEC has repeatedly shown to be untrue.

---

[13] *See* A Resource Guide to the U.S. Foreign Corrupt Practices Act (Nov. 2012),at 40, .

[14] *See, e.g.*, *In re Watts Water Technologies, Inc.*, SEC Accounting and Auditing Enforcement Release No. 3307 (13 Oct. 2011), Admin. Pro. File. No. 3-14585 (charges under section 13(b)(2)(B) for failure to implement FCPA training for employees); *SEC v. Titan Corp.*, No. 05-0411 (D.D.C. 1 Mar. 2005) (failure to implement an anti-bribery policy); Cease-and-Desist Order, *Smith & Wesson Holding Corporation*, Exchange Act Release No. 72678 (28 July 2014) (failure to conduct due diligence on third parties).

[15] *Supra* note 5.

In the Matter of BHP Billiton Ltd. and BHP Billiton Plc[16]

The effects of the SEC's aggressive application of section 13(b)(2)(B) were felt most recently in a civil action brought by the Commission against BHP Billiton Ltd. in May 2015. Under investigation by the Department of Justice and SEC since 2013, BHP Billiton eventually agreed to pay USD 25 million to resolve allegations that the company violated the books and records and internal controls provisions of the FCPA by providing extravagant hospitality to government officials as part of the company's sponsorship of the 2008 Olympics in Beijing. In 2007 and 2008, BHP Billiton allegedly offered three-to-four-day stays at luxury hotels, tickets to Olympic events, meals, and other items to government officials. Each hospitality package was valued at approximately USD 12,000 to USD 16,000, and some government officials also allegedly received business-class airfare.

Interestingly, BHP Billiton designed a system of controls meant to address the exact bribery risk posed by inviting government officials to the Olympics, developing a specific internal approval process for hospitality surrounding the Games. Business managers were required to complete a hospitality form for any individuals—including government officials—whom they wished to invite, and a cover sheet accompanying the blank forms included a short description of BHP Billiton's anti-bribery policy and urged employees to re-read the section concerning travel, entertainment, and gifts before completing the form. Each completed form then needed to be approved by the country president of the various business units. Finally, a supervisory Ethics Panel was established to provide advice on ethical and compliance matters, including those related to the hospitality program.

Despite putting these measures in place, the company's internal controls were ultimately determined to be insufficient by the SEC. Among the reasons, the SEC noted that the hospitality forms were not subject to any independent legal or compliance review; that some were inaccurate or incomplete; that employees did not receive any specific training on how to complete the forms; and that employees were not required to update the forms based on new information. To many, the BHP Billiton case establishes an alarmingly high

---

[16] Order Instituting Cease-and-Desist Proceedings, *In re BHP Billiton Ltd. and BHP Billiton plc*, Release No. 74998 (20 May 2015), *available at* http://www.sec.gov/news/pressrelease/2015-93.html.

threshold for how the SEC measures the sufficiency of a company's internal controls. While perhaps not perfect, BHP Billiton clearly demonstrated numerous efforts to mitigate against its corruption risks. Given that no two company's internal controls are the same and the SEC is always able to engage in after-the-fact analysis relating to financial irregularities, many compliance officers have been left to wonder whether their companies' internal controls could similarly be deemed insufficient.

Complying with the Internal Controls Provision of the FCPA

Companies subject to the internal controls provision of the FCPA must operate in an increasingly difficult regulatory landscape. The combination of the SEC's willingness to apply section 13(b)(2)(B) to non-bribery cases and the fact that companies are increasingly held to a compliance "best practices" standard has created an especially high bar. And until cases like BHP Billiton are litigated in court, the SEC is likely to continue to push for this more expansive reading of the provision.

Given these challenges, companies need to ensure that their internal controls systems are sufficiently robust to meet the SEC's heightened scrutiny. Below are some of the ways companies are meeting this challenge, some of which will be very familiar

- Establishing a clear anti-bribery policy and related procedures;

- Implementing a third party due diligence program that adequately vets and monitors third party business partners;

- Conducting third party audits and reviewing third party outlays that may create bribery risks (e.g. excessive commissions to third parties);

- Ensuring that audits are conducted in accordance with Generally Accepted Auditing Standards and embedding compliance checks into periodic internal audits;

- Cross-training compliance and accounting teams on bribery-related issues;

- Conducting company-wide risk assessments, including the determination of significant accounts, the selection of controls to test, and establishing the evidence necessary for a given control.

- Requiring that the risk assessment produce insight as to the likelihood of bribery risks occurring, the strength of the company's internal controls, and any residual risk that may remain;

- Reviewing procedures related to transfer of funds, such as approvals, authorizations, reconciliations, and segregation of duties;

- Reviewing procedures regarding opening bank accounts and maintaining up-to-date records for all company ledger accounts;

- Reviewing invoices for irregularities, falsehoods, misstatements or other potential fraudulent activities;

- Reviewing procedures for proper recording of all payments—including facilitation payments—on company books; and

- Reviewing procedures related to journal entries and adjustments made in the period-end financial reporting process.

Many companies are already adopting these internal accounting controls; others will need to catch up. But companies are better off dealing with problems in-house than having them disclosed to the SEC. For each of the above recommendations, companies must show not only that the controls have been adequately set up, but that they've been implemented and revised as needed over time. Compliance officers should vigilantly document their efforts to ensure that these controls are working. So long as the SEC's application of the internal controls provision remains unchallenged, the agency will likely continue with its expansive interpretation of the statute. In this environment, taking a proactive approach early on is a company's best defense.

Chapter 5
What You Should Know About Facilitation Payments

The old phrase "the exception that proves the rule" aptly describes the nature of so-called facilitation or "grease" payments in relation to the rules against bribing foreign officials. They are the sole exception explicitly set forth in the United States' FCPA and stand alongside a very small number of affirmative defenses. The exception also appears in other countries' legislation following that trail-blazing 1977 enactment.

Facilitation payments are often thought of as small payments to low-level foreign officials in return for a company getting what it is entitled to. But as a legal doctrine, the concept is more amorphous than that. Since demand for facilitation payments is, at least anecdotally, a relatively common part of doing international business, the facilitation payment exception has the potential to be a mighty exception indeed—perhaps undermining the rules against foreign-official bribery in their entirety. Over time, however, and across various countries, there has been a marked trend toward narrowing the facilitation payment exception. This is done either by removing it from foreign-official bribery laws altogether or, where it remains, by bringing successful enforcement actions in what would otherwise appear to qualify as permissible payments, drawing a prosecutorial line that appears missing from the legislation.

This chapter examines the nature of facilitation payments. After discussing the language of the FCPA, we analyze the judicial decisions and enforcement agency assertions that have functionally narrowed the statutory definition. We then examine how the concept of facilitation payments is addressed outside of U.S. law, from the changing attitudes of the Organisation for Economic Co-operation and Development ("OECD"), to the variety of approaches taken by OECD member countries in their domestic legislation. Finally, the paper examines best practices for companies operating internationally to address the varied legal frameworks—which have nevertheless been consistent in limiting the scope of the facilitation payment exception, nearly to the point of vanishing completely.

Defining Facilitation Payments According to the FCPA

Since its enactment in 1977, the FCPA has always included an exception for facilitation payments. The terms of that exception were substantially amended in 1988, as the previous eleven years had shown that "United States business entities and executives experienced difficulty in discerning a clear line between prohibited bribes and permissible facilitating payments."[1] In the law's current form, a permissible payment for certain governmental actions is referred to as a "facilitating or expediting payment," and defined as:

> [P]ayment to a foreign official, political party, or party official the purpose of which is to expedite or to secure the performance of a routine governmental action by a foreign official, political party, or party official.[2]

"Routine governmental action" is further defined in two ways. First, permissively: providing a non-exhaustive list of types of activities performed by foreign officials for which payment may be given. Second, prohibitively: identifying certain actions performed by foreign officials that do not qualify as "routine."

The permissive examples all require that the action be one "which is ordinarily and commonly performed by a foreign official," and either included among the following specified examples or "of a similar nature":[3]

1. Obtaining permits, licenses and documents qualifying the person to do business in a foreign country;

---

[1] S. Rep. No. 100-85, at 53 (1987).

[2] 15 U.S.C. §§ 78dd-1(b), 78dd-2(b), 78dd-3(b).

[3] 15 U.S.C. §§ 78dd-1(f)(3)(A), 78dd-2(h)(4)(A), 78dd-3(f)(4)(A).

2.   Processing governmental papers, such as visas and work orders;

3.   Providing police protection, mail pick-up and delivery, or scheduling inspections associated with contract performance or inspections related to transit of goods across the country;

4.   Providing phone service, power and water supply, loading or unloading cargo, or protecting perishable products or commodities from deterioration.[4]

On the "prohibited" (non-"routine") side are government contracting decisions, including both the decision itself ("whether, or on what terms, to award new business to or to continue business with a particular party")[5] and any influencing of the decision ("any action taken by a foreign official involved in the decision-making process to encourage a decision to award new business to or continue business with a particular party").[6]

Several facets of this definition are worthy of note, as they may conflict with the general perception of permissible facilitation payments. First, the definition contains no requirement that a facilitation payment be of low value, or that it be something paid routinely or repeatedly. Nowhere in the language of the FCPA is there a basis for concluding that large-value payments cannot constitute facilitation payments, as long as they are for a specified "routine governmental action."

This misperception may have arisen from the requirement that facilitation payments be for "ordinarily and commonly performed" actions. If an action is common, one might reason, then multiple foreign officials are likely to perform it routinely, thereby pushing down the value of any single occurrence and, with it, the cost of facilitating the act. Alternatively, the perception may be derived from the examples of the sorts of actions covered by the exception: things such as the provision of utilities, permits or licenses which, being relatively inexpensive governmental functions in most countries, would not be expected to attract high facilitation payments. Nevertheless, all ra-

---

[4] *Id.*

[5] 15 U.S.C. §§ 78dd-1(f)(3)(B), 78dd-2(h)(4)(B), 78dd-3(f)(4)(B).

[6] *Id.*

tionales notwithstanding, the statutory language within the FCPA, as outlined above, contains no value- or frequency-based criteria for distinguishing bribery from a lawful facilitation payment. According to the plain text, there is no requirement that facilitation payments be repeated or of low value.

Facilitation payments are sometimes also perceived as a narrow exception to the otherwise strong prohibitions on bribery in the FCPA. As discussed below, this may effectively be true as a result of historical patterns of enforcement. In strictly statutory terms, however, facilitation payments are actually defined quite broadly. For one thing, the official actions for which facilitation payments are explicitly lawfully are ones that companies typically encounter very regularly. Inspections relating to transit of goods, loading or unloading, and obtaining visas, permits and licenses are all activities that companies trading abroad will routinely navigate, and they can be among the most common areas of interaction between businesses and foreign officials. Given the frequency of these activities, opportunities for facially permissible facilitation payments may be anything but rare.

If the literal scope of the exception is broader than commonly thought, the explicit range of official actions not open to the facilitation-payment exception may be narrower. As discussed above, such actions are essentially limited to government contracting decisions to award business or continue doing business and actions that encourage such decisions. Outside of government contracting, there is no specific limitation on the discretionary or non-discretionary decisions that may allow for a facilitation payment.

Ultimately, the language of the facilitation-payment exception leaves us with many gray areas. How far, for example, does the exception for "processing governmental papers" extend? The qualification "such as visas and work orders" provides little in the way of clarity or limitation. Even where the examples of relevant governmental actions are more specific, the allowance of facilitation payments for actions "of a similar nature" leaves wide room for interpretation.

The FCPA—the template for so many other anti-corruption treaties and laws—has therefore defined facilitation payments as a broad exception to the generally rigorous prohibition on foreign-official bribery. This exception includes situations which businesses are likely to come across frequently, and provides no express limit on the value or frequency of payments. Reading the statute alone, therefore, one might expect to see an expansive facilitation-payment exception relied upon regularly by companies seeking to justify payments that might otherwise be considered bribes. In reality, however, the exception is rarely invoked, and does little or nothing to prevent enforcement agencies from pursuing companies for bribery in arguably applicable situations.

The Role of Facilitation Payments in FCPA Enforcement

There are two primary ways the U.S. courts and prosecuting agencies charged with enforcing the FCPA have narrowed the effective scope of the facilitation payments exception. First, by limiting the types of governmental actions for which facilitation payment may lawfully be paid; second, by pursuing companies under the books and records provisions of the FCPA for inaccurate recording of otherwise lawful facilitation payments.

Limiting the types of governmental action occasioning facilitation payments

By expanding the class of government actions for which facilitation payments may not be made—above and beyond decisions on government contracting—recent judicial determinations have narrowed the facilitation payment exception as a whole. This is most clearly seen in the case of *United States v. Kay*, decided in 2004 by the U.S. Court of Appeals for the Fifth Circuit.[7] The U.S. Department of Justice ("DOJ") had indicted the defendants for their actions on behalf of American Rice, Inc. in allegedly bribing Haitian customs officials to accept false bills of lading that understated by one-third the quantity of rice shipped to Haiti in order to reduce the company's import duties.[8] Although the case predominantly concerned the business nexus test relative to the FCPA's anti-bribery provisions, when examining the legislative history and Congressional intent behind the Act the court also addressed the facilitation payments exception. The court noted that in 1977,

---

[7] 359 F.3d 738 (5th Cir. 2004).

[8] *Kay*, slip op. at 4.

> Congress sought to prohibit the type of bribery that
> (1) prompts officials to misuse their discretionary
> authority and (2) disrupts market efficiency and
> United States foreign relations, at the same time
> recognizing that smaller payments intended to ex-
> pedite ministerial actions should remain outside of
> the scope of the statute.[9]

While acknowledging its legislative rationale, the court nevertheless characterized "the grease exception" as a "narrow category," finding that Congress had intended "to cast an otherwise wide net over foreign bribery" and "prohibit all other illicit payments that are intended to influence non-trivial official foreign action".[10]

In concluding that the 1988 amendments to the FCPA "illustrate an intention by Congress to identify very limited exceptions" to the law's scope,[11] the *Kay* court opened the way toward the now-familiar understanding of facilitation payments as low-value exchanges involving trivial, non-discretionary official actions. By more strictly construing the types of official actions that can attract facilitation payments, the case substantially narrowed the facilitation payment exception as a whole.

This aspect of *Kay* was not unsupported by previous judicial interpretations. In the 1989 case of *United States v. Duran*,[12] the defendant was charged with violating the FCPA by making payments to officials in the Dominican Republic to release an airplane that was seized on the erroneous allegations that it had been used for smuggling narcotics. All court proceedings in the Dominican Republic were concluded in the defendant's favor and the aircraft was no longer subject to any legal restraint. The defendant then allegedly paid USD 15,000 to Dominican officials to have the plane released. The prosecution argued that the payment was a bribe. The District Court granted the defendant's motion for acquittal, reasoning as follows:

> He was led to believe that neither the Dominican
> Republic nor any other government held any legal

---

[9] *Id.* at 18.

[10] *Id.* at 23–24.

[11] *Id.* at 25–26.

[12] Case No. 89-00802 (S.D. Fla. 21 Nov. 1989).

claim to or right in the aircraft. He understood that it was simply a straightforward matter of expediting the release of an aircraft on behalf of the owner. Any intended payment was simply for the purpose of hurrying along a bureaucratic process. The purpose of the alleged intended payment was to expedite a routine governmental action.[13]

Just as in *Kay*, the *Duran* case rested on whether the nature of the official action was discretionary or ministerial (i.e. non-discretionary), the decision this time coming down in favor of the defendant. One wonders whether the court would reach the same decision today. The release of an aircraft is not among the actions expressly covered by the FCPA's 1988 amendment, and the payment lacked the other commonly recognized hallmarks of a "grease" payment, such as low value and triviality of official action. The repeated emphasis in *Kay* on the narrowness of the facilitation payment exception seems at odds with the *Duran* court's conclusion. The *Duran* court also gave significant weight to the defendant's subjective belief regarding the nature of the governmental action for which he was making payment. But the analysis in *Kay* suggests that whether an official action is discretionary is an objective matter to be determined by the courts.

A more recent discussion of the facilitation payment exception can be found in *United States v. Duperval*,[14] in which the Eleventh Circuit adopts the narrow approach set forth in *Kay*. The defendant, an assistant director at a publicly owned Haitian telecommunications company called Teleco, was charged with money laundering in connection with his receipt of payments that were illicit under the FCPA. The payments were allegedly rewards and kickbacks for helping private companies renew their contracts and slash their payment obligations toward Teleco. The defendant argued that these qualified as facilitation payments, but the court considered it far-fetched that the administration of a multi-million dollar government contract with a private vendor could be deemed a "routine" government action. Not only is it not similar to those listed in the FCPA, but to

---

[13] *Id.*

[14] *United States v. Duperval*, 777 F.3d 1324 (11th Cir. 2015).

find otherwise would defeat the purpose of the FCPA's anti-bribery provisions.[15]

Aside from judicial determinations, U.S. enforcement agencies have taken a consistently dim view of the facilitation payment exception in their enforcement actions—a significant trend in interpreting the governing legislation. One prominent example is the non-prosecution agreement between the DOJ and Wabtec in 2008 following allegations that the company had made improper payments to the government of India for railway construction contracts.[16] The agreement references payments that, on their face, fall within the list of facilitation payment exceptions, including monthly payments of USD 31.50 for regular value added tax administration, inspection charges averaging between USD 67 and USD 358 each, and obtaining contractually-required certificates of conformity for its products.[17] Although such payments seem to fall squarely within the facilitation payment exception, the DOJ does not appear to treat them as such.

Similarly, in 2015 the United States Securities and Exchange Commission ("SEC") pursued a case against two Noble Corporation employees (Mr. Jackson and Mr. Ruehlen),[18] alleging that the defendants had bribed Nigerian officials for temporary import permits for rigs and, in doing so, falsified internal accounting records and compliance controls. In its summary judgment motion, the SEC asserted that the application of the facilitation payment exception depended on whether the relevant official action was considered discretionary under applicable foreign law. This argument aims to narrow the scope of official actions subject to the exception, not only by excluding all discretionary decisions (as opposed to ministerial actions), but more importantly by requiring objective determination of this fact by reference to the law of the foreign official's country. This is in marked contrast to the court's ruling in *Duran* that relied heavily on the defendant's subjective understanding of the nature of the official action.

---

[15] *Id.* at 1334–35.

[16] *SEC v. Westinghouse Air Brake Tech. Corp.*, Case No. 08-cv-706 (E.D. Pa.), Litigation Release No. 20457 (14 Feb. 2008).

[17] *Id.*; *see also* E. Strauss, " 'Easing Out' The FCPA Facilitation Payment Exception", 93 Boston Univ. L. Rev. 235 (2013), at 252–53.

[18] *SEC v. Jackson & Ruehlen*, Case No. 12-cv-563 (S.D. Tex., 2015).

This brief review of some of the judicial determinations and U.S. enforcement agency assertions regarding facilitation payments shows that the seemingly broad statutory language has been interpreted as offering only a narrow exception to the sweeping anti-bribery provisions of the FCPA. This narrowing effect is achieved primarily by a restrictive interpretation of the type of governmental actions that may bring a payment within the exception, based on qualities inherent to the governmental act. As demonstrated by *Kay*, these interpretations rely largely on congressional intent rather than statutory language. Comparing the findings and tenor of the Duran judgment in 1989 with the outcomes in *Duperval* and *Jackson & Ruehlen* in 2015, we can see a trend toward an increasingly narrow interpretation of the facilitation payment exception.

Facilitation Payments and the Books and Records Provisions of the FCPA

Since the facilitation payment exception relates only to the FCPA's anti-bribery provisions, companies may still be pursued by the authorities for breaches of the Act's books and records provisions for transactions that look very similar to facilitation payments.

In 2007, the SEC settled with Dow Chemical Company over the actions of its fifth-tier subsidiary in India.[19] The allegations concerned accounting failures, some involving the improper bestowal of gifts and hospitality for commercial advantage, but others relating to what were arguably facilitation payments. The subsidiary needed registrations and licenses for its agricultural chemical products from India's Central Insecticides Board. It allegedly paid USD 39,700 to "expedite the registration of three [of those] products."[20] The SEC's enforcement action focused not on the legality of the payments (including the expediting payment), but instead on the allegation that they were improperly recorded in Dow's books, in violation of the FCPA's accounting provisions. Dow ended up paying a USD 325,000 civil penalty to resolve the matter.

In 2009, the SEC reached a settlement agreement and the DOJ concluded a non-prosecution agreement with Helmerich & Payne, Inc.

---

[19] *Dow Chem. Co.*, Accounting and Auditing Enforcement Release No. 2554 (13 Feb. 2007).

[20] *Id.*

The case centered on the actions of the company's Argentine and Venezuelan subsidiaries in allegedly making payments to customs officials to facilitate the shipment of drilling equipment into and out of those countries. In the SEC action, the cease and desist order concedes that some "payments were made with the purpose and effect of avoiding potential delays typically associated with the international transportation of drilling parts."[21] Although the SEC characterizes these payments as 'improper', the basis for seeking the cease and desist order was the FCPA's books and records provisions.[22] The parallel DOJ enforcement action acknowledged that the company made some payments "to facilitate the performance of routine governmental action", but criticized the company for improperly recording these payments within its accounts in order to conceal the true nature and purpose of the payments.[23] The SEC settled its action in respect of the alleged books and records violation—including in relation to those payments that would appear to be facilitation payments—in return for the company paying approximately USD 320,000 in disgorgement and USD 55,000 in prejudgment interest.[24]

In a 2010 complaint against Joe Summers—an employee of Pride International, Inc.—the SEC went so far as to allege violations of both the FCPA's anti-bribery provision and its books and records provision in a case where some of the payments arguably fell within the facilitation payment exception.[25] The complaint included allegations regarding authorization of a single payment of USD 30,000 to a mid-level Venezuelan state-owned oil company employee who was "holding up the payment of funds owed to Pride Foramer Venezuela" (a subsidiary of Pride International, Inc.).[26] Expediting the payment of sums due under a contract would seem to be the sort of thing that would be encompassed within the facilitation payments exception, but that didn't prevent the SEC from alleging that the payment constituted bribery, as it was made "for purposes of securing

---

[21] *In re Helmerich & Payne, Inc.*, Administrative Proceeding File No. 3-13565, at 2.

[22] *Id.*

[23] *See* DOJ non-prosecution agreement, Appendix A at 4, para. 16, *available at* https://www.justice.gov/sites/default/files/criminal-fraud/legacy/2011/02/16/06-29-09helmerich-agree.pdf.

[24] *In Re: Helmerich & Payne, Inc.*, Administrative Proceeding File No. 3-13565, at 5.

[25] *SEC v. Joe Summers*, 4:10-cv-02786 (S.D. Tex., complaint filed 5 Aug. 2010).

[26] *Id.* at 5.

an improper advantage in receiving payment" from the state-owned Venezuelan oil company,[27] while also alleging a books-and-records violation based on the same facts.[28]

In each of these cases, the targeted payments could be considered textbook examples of facilitation payments; some are even recognized as such by the enforcement agencies. Yet the companies still faced enforcement actions and significant civil penalties by virtue of the books and records provisions of the FCPA. This use of the FCPA's accounting provisions to pursue companies for actions that might be deemed permissible as facilitation payments arguably frustrates the legislative intent—Congress's recognition, as described in *Kay*, "that smaller payments intended to expedite ministerial actions should remain outside of the scope of the statute."[29] Whether or not such prosecutions conform to the Act's underlying purpose, they demonstrate a stark reality for companies conducting international business: in practice, the facilitation payment exception offers essentially no protection with respect to the FCPA's accounting provisions.

Facilitation Payments in Laws Outside the United States

Given the multi-national nature of many companies' business, compliance and ethics officers must attend not only to the FCPA but also to the anti-bribery legislation of other jurisdictions. This includes laws addressing transnational bribery as well as laws targeting bribery domestically, as the latter not only govern the actions of a company's subsidiaries operating or incorporated in such countries, but may also be relevant to determining whether an official act is discretionary or not.

The OECD Convention

The 1997 OECD Convention (the "Convention") initially permitted facilitation payments, though somewhat ambivalently. According to the Convention's commentary:

---

[27] *Id.*

[28] *Id.* at 8.

[29] *Kay*, slip op. at 18.

Small "facilitation" payments do not constitute payments made "to obtain or retain business or other improper advantage" within the meaning of [the Convention] and, accordingly, are also not an offence. Such payments, which, in some countries, are made to induce public officials to perform their functions, such as issuing licenses or permits, are generally illegal in the foreign country concerned. Other countries can and should address this corrosive phenomenon by such means as support for programmes of good governance. However, criminalisation by other countries does not seem a practical or effective complementary action.[30]

So, while it recognizes the practice of facilitation payments as "corrosive" and "generally illegal" under domestic law, the Convention declines to bring them within the scope of its own prohibitions. At the same time, this commentary offers relatively little substance regarding the nature of such payments, or how in practice to distinguish them from prohibited bribes. It does, however, insert the qualifier "small" which is absent from the FCPA.

This ambivalence was somewhat mitigated in the OECD Council's 2009 Recommendation.[31] Continuing to highlight the "corrosive effect" of facilitation payments on sustainable economic development and the rule of law,[32] the Recommendation goes further by encouraging Member countries to "periodically review their policies and approach on small facilitation payments in order to effectively combat the phenomenon"[33] and "encourage companies to prohibit or discourage the use of small facilitation payments in internal company controls". [34] The Recommendation also urges countries to tackle the

---

[30] OECD, Commentaries on the Convention on Combating Bribery of Foreign Public Officials in International Business Transactions (adopted by the Negotiating Conference 21 Nov. 1997), at para. 9.

[31] OECD, Recommendation of the Council for Further Combating Bribery of Foreign Public Officials in International Business Transactions (adopted by the Council 26 Nov. 2009).

[32] Id. at para. VI.

[33] Id. at para. VI(i).

[34] Id. at para. VI(ii).

demand side of facilitation payments by "rais[ing] awareness of their public officials on their domestic bribery and solicitation laws".[35]

Between 1997 and 2009, then, the OECD appears, like the U.S. courts and enforcement agencies, to have limited the practical significance of the facilitation payment exception—not so much by narrowing the exception's reach, but rather by more explicitly denouncing the practice.

Other Countries' Legislation

The global spread of foreign-official bribery laws is often understood to have originated with the U.S. FCPA, moving therefrom to the OECD Convention and, subsequently, into the domestic legislation of OECD member countries and beyond. Given the OECD's initial ambivalence on the issue, it is unsurprising to see a certain initial variation in the approach taken to facilitation payments by individual OECD member countries. The following countries' legislation has been chosen for review as representing a spectrum of such approaches and attitudes.

On one end of the spectrum are countries like Australia that have incorporated the facilitation payment exception and show no current signs of amending their legislation, though they have flirted with the idea. Australia adopted the facilitation payment exception in much the same terms as the 1988 version of the FCPA,[36] and even permitted income tax breaks for such payments, while also imposing certain record-keeping requirements. Reviewing Australia's implementation of the Convention in 2012, the OECD Working Group noted concerns about the country's handling of the exception:

> Facilitation payments appear to be frequently equated with any bribes of small value. Often overlooked is the requirement that such payments must be made to secure routine governmental action of a minor nature that does not result in the obtaining of a business advantage.[37]

---

[35] *Id.* at para. VII.

[36] *See* Criminal Code Act 1995, Division 70.

[37] OECD Working Group Phase 3 Report on Implementing the OECD Anti-Bribery convention in Australia (Oct. 2012), at 10.

The review also suggested that facilitation payments by Australian companies were common, particularly in the Asia-Pacific region.[38] In its 2015 follow-up report, the Working Group expressed concern about whether the Australian authorities had adequately publicized the differences between permissible facilitation payments and unlawful bribes.[39] The legislature has undertaken further inquiries, but there has not yet been any substantive revision to the law. For the time being, therefore, Australia seems to have bucked the international trend of narrowing the scope of the facilitation payment exception.

In New Zealand, the Crimes Act 1961, as amended in 2001, provided an exception for payments to foreign officials where, first, the value of the benefit is small and, second, the payment is for the sole or primary purpose of expediting performance by a foreign public official of a routine government action.[40] Notably the phrase "facilitation payment" is avoided in the legislation and the low-value requirement is included as a specific hallmark of the type of permissible payment. When this law was passed in 2001, it defined "routine government action" negatively as not including: decisions about awarding new business; decisions about continuing existing business; decisions about the terms of new or existing business; and decisions outside the scope of the ordinary duties of that official.[41] New Zealand has recently narrowed the facilitation payment exception further through its passage of the Crimes Amendment Act 2015. This Act added an additional category of exclusions from the facilitation payment exception, namely that "routine government action" may not include "any action that provides an undue material benefit to a person who makes a payment, or any undue disadvantage to any other person."[42] The reason this amendment is so wide ranging is neatly explained by the guidance to companies issued by the New Zealand Ministry of Justice before the 2015 amendments were passed:

---

[38] *Id.* ("There is a perception that Australian companies may be making facilitation payments and that the practice may be prevalent, at least in certain regions… especially in the Asia-Pacific region").

[39] OECD Working Group, "Australia: Follow-up to the Phase 3 Report and Recommendations" (Apr. 2015), at 5.

[40] Crimes Act 1961 as amended by the Crimes (Bribery of Foreign Public Officials) Amendments Act 2001, at § 105C(1).

[41] *Id.* at § 105C(3).

[42] *Id.* at § 105C(1), as amended by the Crimes Amendment Act 2015. s.6(2) and s.6(3).

Facilitation payments will be illegal in most countries where they are made. Therefore, if you pay them, you will likely break the law in the foreign country where you are doing business. Further, any payment that is illegal in the country where it occurs will likely provide an undue material benefit to the payer, and therefore fall outside the scope of New Zealand's exception.[43]

The guidance concludes that "as a matter of best practice, businesses should develop procedures and controls to prohibit [facilitation payments]."

Canada's foreign-official bribery law originally included a facilitation payment exception, but subsequent legislation is set to repeal rather than merely narrow it. The Corruption of Foreign Public Officials Act (CFPOA) of 1999 permitted facilitation payments in almost exactly the same terms as the 1988 version of the FCPA.[44] However, on 19 June 2013 the Canadian Parliament passed the Fighting Corruption Act, which included a provision for the complete elimination of the facilitation payment exception.[45] These amendments, however, are only to come into force on a date to be determined by the Canadian cabinet. At the time of writing, almost four years since the passage of the Fighting Corruption Act, no such date has been set.[46] The reason for this may be to enable Canadian businesses to adjust to the significant legislative shift.

In a very similar vein to Canada, South Korea, which originally permitted facilitation payments as part of its Foreign Bribery Prevention in International Business Transactions Act, amended the law and deleted the facilitation payment exception in 2014.[47] In contrast

---

[43] New Zealand Ministry of Justice Publication, "Facilitation Payments and New Zealand's anti-bribery laws" (2015), at 1.

[44] Corruption of Foreign Public Officials Act S.C. 1998 c.34, at s.3(4) and s.3(5) (in force from 14 Feb. 1999).

[45] 2013, c.26, s.3(2).

[46] *See* Canadian Department of Justice, Consolidated Laws, S.C. 1998. c.34 (amendments not in force), available at http://laws-lois.justice.gc.ca/eng/acts/C-45.2/nifnev.html.

[47] Norton Rose Fulbright, "Business ethics and anti-corruption laws: South Korea" (Sept. 2014), *available at* http://www.nortonrosefulbright.com/knowledge/publications/121085/business-ethics-and-anti-corruption-laws-south-korea#section5.

to Canada, these amendments are not merely pending, but have actually come into force.

Uniquely, the United Kingdom has never adopted a legislative exception for facilitation payments, either in the Bribery Act 2010 or under pre-existing legislation.[48] As such, facilitation payments have always been considered illegal bribes. The waters were somewhat muddied when the Ministry of Justice issued guidance in 2011 suggesting that the enforcement agencies had only a limited prosecutorial appetite for facilitation payment cases.[49] This caused the UK Serious Fraud Office ("SFO") to issue further guidance in October 2012, which exhibited a rather harder attitude:

> A facilitation payment is a type of bribe and should be seen as such. . . . Facilitation payments were illegal before the Bribery Act came into force and they are illegal under the Bribery Act, regardless of their size or frequency.[50]

The guidance continued (somewhat in tension with the suggestion in the Ministry of Justice's 2011 publication) that the usual tests would be applied in determining whether or not to prosecute facilitation payment cases, as with any other bribery case. Yet even this apparently unequivocal revised guidance by the SFO left some room for prosecutorial discretion with respect to facilitation payments.[51] In any event, despite a bit of stammering early in the lifetime of the UK Bribery Act, the UK maintains a legislative prohibition on facilitation payments however defined.

The above snapshot demonstrates clear differences in the attitudes of different OECD member countries towards facilitation payments, ranging from complete lawfulness to complete prohibition. Never-

---

[48] *See, e.g.*, United Kingdom's Ministry of Justice, "The Bribery Act 2010, Guidance" (first published 30 Mar. 2011), at para. 45.

[49] *Id.* at para. 46 ("The eradication of facilitation payments is recognized at the national and international level as a long term objective that will require economic and social progress and sustained commitment to the rule of law in those of the world where the problem is most prevalent").

[50] *See* Serious Fraud Office, "Bribery Act: Guidance on adequate procedures, facilitation payments and business expenditure" (Oct. 2012), *available at* https://www.sfo.gov.uk/publications/guidance-policy-and-protocols/bribery-act-guidance/.

[51] *Id.* at "Questions and Answers" ("It would be wrong to say there is no flexibility.").

theless, even across so many different countries with such diverse legal traditions and trading patterns, the trend has only ever been in one direction: towards a narrower role for facilitation payments, whether through mere consideration of narrowing amendments (Australia), actually enacting such amendments (New Zealand), or prohibiting facilitation payments entirely (Canada prospectively; South Korea presently; and the UK perennially). This common narrowing trend mirrors the trend already identified both in the U.S. and in the OECD's 2009 Recommendation.

How Should Companies Respond?

The foregoing analysis demonstrates that, although the statutory language in the FCPA seemingly provides for a commonly occurring and flexibly drafted pragmatic exception to bribery prohibitions, subsequent actions by U.S. judicial and executive actors have significantly curtailed its scope. The same narrowing trend has been observed with respect to international treaty monitoring bodies and other countries around the world—though there remains a level of diversity in the extent to which the exception has been narrowed. Given both the range of current law and the consistent trend away from tolerance of facilitation payments, how can companies remain complaint?

Clearly, enforcement under the FCPA and similar legislation represents a significant and costly risk, to which some companies may react by stubbornly relying on a broad interpretation of the facilitation payment exception. But they do so at their peril. The trend toward narrowing the scope of the facilitation payment exception has happened in so many countries that it has become unavoidable. Companies may be tempted to hedge their bets by continuing to make what they regard as facilitation payments but characterizing such payments as something else. This, however, creates an additional risk of prosecution under the books and records provisions of the FCPA, even for facilitation payments that might otherwise have been deemed valid.

For companies operating in only a few countries internationally, it is possible to conceive of a country-by-country compliance program in which the confines of each individual country's facilitation payment exception are clearly outlined and regular training is given to staff as to what is, and what is not, permissible. However, this approach would require significant monitoring and agility by a company's compliance team, along with ongoing attention to the legality of such payments both in the company's home country and in the country of payment.

Beyond those sorts of logistical issues, seeking to accurately navigate permissible facilitation payments may be a fool's errand when, in fact, the dividing line between legality and illegality is perilously thin and ill-defined. Is it the size of the payment that matters? The exercise of discretion by the foreign official? A list of particularized examples? Situations analogous to such a list? The regularity of the action being performed by the foreign official? The seniority of the foreign official? The value of the action's benefit to the company? The proximity of the action to government contracting? The answers can vary not just among different countries, but at different times within a single country. Given this variety, instituting a country-by-country compliance policy would be a challenge to say the least.

The simplest and most reliable answer is for businesses to avoid facilitation payments altogether by forbidding them in their compliance regimes—allowing the market to complement and complete the narrowing trend seen in the legislation. This is the least risky approach, and one that market forces will naturally favor. It is no coincidence that companies are already choosing this approach. In 2003, TRACE published *The High Cost of Small Bribes*,[52] delineating the business and reputational arguments against facilitation payments, and many companies began to prohibit these risky and corrosive payments around that time. The 2009 recommendation by the OECD Council,[53] and guidance such as that issued by the UK in 2011,[54] foresaw the central role private enterprise would ultimately play in eradicating facilitation payments altogether. From being the exception to the rule, facilitation payments are moving toward being eclipsed by the rule entirely.

---

[52] *Available at* https://www.traceinternational.org/Uploads/PublicationFiles/TheHigh-CostofSmallBribes2015.pdf.

[53] OECD Recommendation, at para. VI (member countries should "encourage companies to prohibit or discourage the use of small facilitation payments in internal company controls, ethics and compliance programmes or measures").

[54] United Kingdom Ministry of Justice, "The Bribery Act 2010, Guidance" (first published 30 Mar. 2011), at para. 46 ("Businesses themselves also have a role to play and the guidance below offers an indication of how the problem may be addressed through the selection of bribery prevention procedures by commercial organizations.").

Chapter 6
What You Should Know About Individual Liability

> The number of individual prosecutions has risen—and that's not an accident. That is quite intentional on the part of the Department. It is our view that to have a credible deterrent effect, people have to go to jail. People have to be prosecuted where appropriate. This is a federal crime. This is not fun and games.[1]

> – Mark Mendelsohn, Former Deputy Chief of the Fraud Section of the U.S. Department of Justice Criminal Division.

With this statement, the DOJ made clear to the world that the United States' largest law enforcement agency considers the prosecution of individuals in corruption cases to be a priority. Over the past eight years, the DOJ has reinforced this commitment by charging dozens of individuals with the violation of bribery-related statutes, including the FCPA. In September 2015, the DOJ formalized its policies regarding the prosecution of individuals with the release of the "Yates Memo," which targets individuals who engage in corporate wrongdoing.[2]

Although the greatest share of FCPA enforcement activity continues to be directed against corporations, individuals must remain vigilant about their personal compliance with the statute. For individuals that work in companies that do business abroad, the risk of liability has increased significantly over the past decade. Certain individuals—executives, directors, sales and marketing managers, agents—face increased risks given the nature of their work, their interactions with government officials, and their supervisory responsibilities. This risk increases dramatically for individuals working on high value

---

[1] "Mendelsohn Says Criminal Bribery Prosecutions Doubled in 2007," 22 Corporate Crime Reporter 36(1) (16 Sept. 2008).

[2] Department of Justice: Sally Quillian Yates, "Memorandum Re Individual Accountability for Corporate Wrongdoing" (9 Sept. 2015), *available at* http://bit.ly/justice-dag.

projects in developing countries where corruption is more prevalent and the pressure to "make a deal" is higher.

Despite the fact that the policies behind the FCPA are fairly straight-forward, the statute's legal framework is complex. This chapter de-codes the unique provisions of the FCPA related to the prosecution of individuals and focuses on the practical implications of recent en-forcement policies and actions.

Individual Liability Under the FCPA's Anti-Bribery Prohibitions

In general, the FCPA prohibits the payment of money or anything of value to a foreign official to influence an act or decision or secure an improper advantage in order to obtain or retain business.[3] It also requires the maintenance of accurate books and records and robust internal controls.[4] These two provisions often work in tandem, pro-hibiting bribery as well as the concealment of bribes in off-book accounts and slush funds.

The FCPA provides several jurisdictional categories of individuals that may be prosecuted for violating the FCPA:

1. Officers, directors, employees or agents of an issuer[5] or do-mestic concern[6] if they make "use of the mails or any means or instrumentality of interstate commerce" in furtherance of an improper payment to a foreign official.[7]

2. Citizens, nationals, or residents of the United States, even if their misconduct occurs entirely outside the United States.[8]

---

[3] 15 U.S.C. §§ 78dd-1 et seq.; A Resource Guide to the U.S. Foreign Corrupt Practices Act ("FCPA Guide"), at 10, *available at* https://www.justice.gov/sites/default/files/crimi-nal-fraud/legacy/2015/01/16/guide.pdf.

[4] 15 U.S.C. § 78m.

[5] "A company is an 'issuer' under the FCPA if it has a class of securities registered under Section 12 of the Exchange Act46 or is required to file periodic and other reports with SEC under Section 15(d) of the Exchange Act." FCPA Guide at 11.

[6] The definition of "domestic concern" includes citizens, nationals, or residents of the United States. 15 U.S.C. § 78dd-2.

[7] 15 U.S.C. §§ 78dd-1(a), 78dd-2(a)).

[8] 15 U.S.C. § 78dd-1(g).

3. Any other person other than an issuer or domestic concern (i.e., foreign nationals) if that person engages in any act in furtherance of a bribe while in the territory of the United States.[9]

The government has construed the prohibition against providing "anything of value" to a foreign official very broadly and does not impose a minimum dollar threshold on the improper gift or payment.[10] There must also be a "business purpose" behind the improper payment. In other words, the payment must be given in order to obtain or retain a business advantage.[11] This doesn't just mean paying a government official to secure a contract. It also encompasses payments provided to, among other things, reduce customs duties, circumvent licensing or zoning approval processes, or reduce tax liabilities.[12]

To violate the statute's anti-bribery prohibitions, "an offer, promise, or authorization of a payment, or a payment, to a government official must be made 'corruptly.'"[13] An act is considered "corrupt" if it is "done voluntarily [a]nd intentionally, and with a bad purpose of accomplishing either an unlawful end or result, or a lawful end or result by some unlawful method or means."[14] This standard is met if, among other things, the payment (or offer, promise, or authorization of the payment) is made for any one of the following four reasons: (1) to influence any act or decision of the foreign official in his official capacity; (2) to induce the foreign official to do or omit to do any act in violation of the official's lawful duty; (3) to induce the foreign official to use his influence with a foreign government or instrumentality to affect or influence any act or decision of government or instrumentality; or (4) to secure any improper advantage.[15]

In *United States v. Liebo*, the U.S. Court of Appeals for the Eighth Circuit squarely addressed the meaning of "corruptly."[16] In *Liebo*, the

---

[9] 15 U.S.C. § 78dd-3.

[10] FCPA Guide at 15.

[11] *Id.* at 12.

[12] *Id.* at 13.

[13] *Id.* at 14.

[14] *United States v. Liebo*, 923 F.2d, 1308 (8th Cir. 1991).

[15] 15 U.S.C. §§ 78dd-1 *et seq.*

[16] *Liebo*, 923 F.2d at 1312.

vice president of a large aerospace firm had bought plane tickets for the honeymoon of a family member of a government official from Niger. Liebo's company sought contracts with the Ministry of Defense and the tickets were given to the cousin of a government official who could (and eventually did) influence the contract award. Liebo argued that the tickets were merely a personal gift and claimed that this negated a finding that he was acting corruptly when buying the tickets. The Eighth Circuit rejected this argument, explaining that there was sufficient evidence of corrupt intent where, among other factors, the tickets were given to the cousin of an official involved in the contract approval process shortly before the contract was approved. Liebo also improperly recorded the tickets in the company's books and records as "commission payments."[17]

Notably, FCPA liability may attach even if the corrupt act does not succeed in its purpose. As the DOJ has explained:

> [A]s long as the offer, promise, authorization, or payment is made corruptly, the actor need not know the identity of the recipient; the attempt is sufficient. Thus, an executive who authorizes others to pay "whoever you need to" in a foreign government to obtain a contract has violated the FCPA—even if no bribe is ultimately offered or paid.[18]

In addition to possessing corrupt intent, an individual must have knowledge of the wrongdoing. The FCPA covers payments made to "any person, while knowing that all or a portion of such money or thing of value will be offered, given, or promised, directly or indirectly, to any foreign official."[19] Liability may be imposed on any person with actual knowledge, with an awareness or firm belief that an event is likely to occur, or who avoids knowledge of corrupt acts through "willful blindness."[20] Thus, the statute is applicable "not only

---

[17] Liebo was "sentenced to 18 months in prison, suspended with three years' probation, with 60 days of home confinement and 600 hours of community service." Richard L. Cassin, "May it Please the Court" (1 May 2008), *available at* http://www.fcpablog.com/blog/2008/5/2/may-it-please-the-court.html.

[18] FCPA Guide at 14 (citing Complaint, *SEC v. Innospec, Inc.*, No. 10-cv-448 (D.D.C. 18 Mar. 2010)).

[19] 15 U.S.C. § 78dd-1 *et seq.*

[20] FCPA Guide at 22 (citing H.R. Rep. No. 100-576, at 920 (1988)).

on those with actual knowledge of wrongdoing, but also on those who purposefully avoid actual knowledge." [21]

The FCPA's broad knowledge standard (coupled with its prohibition against both direct and indirect payments) empowers the government to prosecute individuals that try to conceal payments through the use of third parties or other intermediaries (i.e., consultants, agents, distributors, joint venture partners, etc.). For example, in *United States v. Kozeny*,[22] the U.S. Court of Appeals for the Second Circuit upheld the conviction of Frederic Bourke for his role in a conspiracy to violate the FCPA's anti-bribery provisions by approving payments to government officials in Azerbaijan in an attempt to influence the privatization of the country's state oil company. In its discussion of the FCPA's "knowledge" standard, the Second Circuit referred to evidence and testimony from the trial indicating that, among other things, Bourke (1) knew corruption was pervasive in Azerbaijan, (2) knew his business partner, nicknamed the "Pirate of Prague," had a reputation for corruption, (3) created companies to shield himself and other investors from potential liability, and (4) during a conference call, expressed concerns that his business partner and company were bribing officials.

The Second Circuit made clear that there was abundant evidence that Bourke had "serious concerns about the legality" of his partner's business practices "and worked to avoid learning exactly what [he] was doing." When viewing the totality of the evidence, the Second Circuit found that "a rational juror could conclude that Bourke deliberately avoided confirming his suspicions" about his business partner's bribes. Bourke was sentenced to 366 days in prison and ordered to pay a USD 1 million fine.

Although corporations and individuals are generally subject to the same standards under the FCPA, there is an additional requirement applicable only to the prosecution of individuals. Specifically, the government must demonstrate that an individual has acted "willfully" when bribing a foreign official. The FCPA does not define the term "willfully," but it has been construed as connoting an "act committed voluntarily and purposefully, and with a bad purpose, i.e.,

---

[21] *Id.*

[22] 667 F.3d 122 (2d Cir. 2011).

with 'knowledge that [a defendant] was doing a 'bad' act under the general rules of law.'"[23] Moreover, to prove a "willful" violation of the FCPA's anti-bribery prohibitions, the Government "must prove that the defendant acted with knowledge that his conduct was unlawful."[24] The FCPA does not, however, "require the government to prove that a defendant was specifically aware of the FCPA or knew that his conduct violated the FCPA."[25]

Individual Liability Under the FCPA's Accounting & Internal Controls Provisions

Individuals may also be held civilly and criminally liable for failing to comply with the FCPA's accounting (or "books and records") and internal controls provisions. The provisions apply to foreign and domestic issuers of securities, and to their officers, directors, employees and agents.[26]

To hold an individual liable for civilly violating the FCPA's books and records and internal controls provisions, the SEC must demonstrate that the individual "knowingly circumvent[ed] or knowingly fail[ed] to implement a system of internal accounting controls or knowingly falsif[ied] any book, record, or account" described in 15 U.S.C. § 78m(b)(2).[27]

For example, in 2006, the SEC settled an enforcement action against David Pillor—the former Senior Vice President for Sales and Marketing (and member of the board of directors) of InVision Technologies, Inc.[28] The SEC alleged that InVision's sales agents and distributors made payments to foreign officials in China, Thailand and the Philippines to obtain or retain business for the company. At the

---

[23] FCPA Guide at 14 (citing *United States v. Kay*, 513 F.3d 432, 448 (5th Cir. 2007)).

[24] *Id.* (citing *Bryan v. United States*, 524 U.S. 184, 191–92 (1998)).

[25] *Id.* (citing *Kay*, 513 F.3d at 447-48).

[26] An "issuer" is a U.S. or foreign company, or an officer, employee, agent or stockholder thereof, that either issues securities (or American Depositary Receipts) or must file reports with the SEC. 15 U.S.C. § 78dd-1(a).

[27] 15 U.S.C. § 78m(b)(5). To hold an individual criminally liable for violating the accounting and internal controls provisions of the FCPA, the government must also demonstrate that an individual acted "willfully" in violating these provisions. See 15 U.S.C. § 78ff(a).

[28] *SEC v. David M. Pillor*, No. 1:06-C-4906 (N.D. Cal. 2006); SEC Litigation Release No. 19803 (15 Aug. 2006).

time of the transactions, Pillor received email communications from a regional sales manager suggesting that the company's third parties were intending to make improper payments to foreign officials. InVision subsequently paid the invoices for these transactions and improperly recorded the payments as legitimate business expenses. The SEC claimed that Pillor aided and abetted InVision's failure to establish and maintain a system of internal controls adequate to detect and prevent the company's violations of the FCPA. He also indirectly caused the falsification of InVision's books and records. In settling the matter with the SEC, Pillor agreed to, among other things, pay a USD 65,000 civil penalty.

Liability for civil violations of the books and records and internal controls provisions of the FCPA may also be triggered based on an individual's position as a "control person" within the company. The SEC relied on this theory in a 2009 enforcement action involving two senior executives of Nature's Sunshine Product, Inc., a manufacturer of nutritional and personal care products.[29] The SEC alleged that the company bribed customs officials and purchased false documentation to conceal the improper payments. The SEC charged the executives as "control persons"—alleging that they had knowledge of the misconduct due to their supervisory positions. Notably, the complaint never claims that the executives participated in or knew of the misconduct—the allegations are based on a "failure to adequately supervise" theory.

Penalties for violating the FCPA

The penalties for violating the FCPA can be severe. An individual criminal conviction carries a fine of up to USD 250,000 and five years in prison.[30] Civil penalties can go as high as USD 16,000 per violation.[31] Criminal violations of the accounting and internal control provisions may result in a fine of up to USD 5 million and twenty years in prison per violation.[32] Civil violations of these provisions

---

[29] *SEC v. Nature's Sunshine Products, Inc. et al.*, No. 09-0672 (D. Utah 2009); SEC Litigation Release No. 21162 (31 July 2009).

[30] 15 U.S.C. §§ 78dd-2(g)(2)(A), 78dd-3(e)(2)(A), 78ff(c)(2)(A); 18 U.S.C. § 3571.

[31] 15 U.S.C. §§ 78dd-2(g)(2)(B), 78dd-3(e)(2)(B), 78ff(c)(2)(B); *see also* 17 C.F.R. § 201.1004.

[32] 15 U.S.C. § 78ff(a).

may result in a fine of USD 7,500 to 150,000 per violation.[33] In addition, the "Sentence of fine" statute allows the government to fine persons up to twice the gross pecuniary gain or loss resulting from the corrupt payment. [34]Moreover, an individual's fines may not be paid by his or her employer.[35]

Prioritizing the Prosecution of Individuals: The Yates Memo & DOJ Disclosure Pilot Program

While the government has spent the past decade emphasizing the importance of prosecuting individual FCPA violators, in 2015 and 2016, the DOJ formalized this strategy by announcing two new policies that will likely have a dramatic impact on the number of individuals investigated, charged and convicted of violating the FCPA.

The Yates Memo

In September 2015, DOJ Deputy Attorney General Sally Quillian Yates issued a memorandum to all DOJ attorneys, titled "Individual Accountability for Corporate Wrongdoing" (the "Yates Memo").[36] The Yates Memo formalizes the DOJ's goal of "combat[ing] corporate misconduct" by seeking "accountability from individuals who perpetrate the wrongdoing." The policies outlined in the Yates Memo heighten the risk of individual liability for criminal prosecution or civil action. The Yates Memo identifies six "key steps" to enable DOJ prosecutors "to most effectively pursue the individuals responsible for corporate wrongs." Those steps are:

1. "To be eligible for any cooperation credit, corporations must provide to the [DOJ] all relevant facts about the individuals involved in the corporate misconduct."

2. "Both criminal and civil corporate investigations should focus on individuals from the inception of the investigation."

---

[33] 15 U.S.C. § 78u(d)(3); *see also* 17 C.F.R. § 201.1004.

[34] 18 U.S.C. § 3571(d).

[35] 15 U.S.C. §§ 78dd-2(g)(3), 78dd-3(e)(3), 78ff(c)(3).

[36] *Supra* note 2.

3. "Criminal and civil attorneys handling corporate investigations should be in routine communication with one another."

4. "Absent extraordinary circumstances, no corporate resolution will provide protection from criminal or civil liability for any individuals."

5. "Corporate cases should not be resolved without a clear plan to resolve related individual cases before the statute of limitations expires and declinations as to individuals in such cases must be memorialized."

6. "Civil attorneys should consistently focus on individuals as well as the company and evaluate whether to bring suit against an individual based on considerations beyond that individual's ability to pay."

The steps outlined in the Yates Memo make clear that corporations must assist the DOJ with the prosecution of culpable individuals to be eligible for any cooperation credit. This will incentivize corporations to turn over individuals to preserve the best possible deal for the company. In turn, this could have a chilling effect on company employees who may fear that they will be implicating themselves if they cooperate with an investigation. In turn, this may force them to choose between remaining loyal to the company by cooperating or face potential criminal or civil liability. This may also create an increasing number of conflicts of interest for companies, requiring the retention of separate representation for certain individuals.

DOJ FCPA Enforcement "Pilot Program"

In April 2016, the DOJ underlined its commitment to prosecuting individuals by launching a one-year "pilot program" designed to encourage companies to voluntarily self-disclose potential violations and identify the individuals who engaged in wrongdoing. Although the pilot program aims to address several policy goals, it also serves as a reminder of the DOJ's renewed commitment to individual prosecutions. The pilot program is outlined in a memorandum titled:

"The Fraud Section's Foreign Corrupt Practices Act Enforcement Plan and Guidance" (the "Guidance").[37]

The Guidance "sets forth the requirements for a company to qualify for credit for voluntary self-disclosure, cooperation, and timely and appropriate remediation under this pilot program, including exceptions to the general rules." The requirements include:

- Voluntary Disclosure in FCPA Matters;

- Full Cooperation in FCPA Matters;

- Timely and Appropriate Remediation in FCPA Matters.

The Guidance highlights several factors involving individuals that will impact potential cooperation credit. For example, in order for a disclosure to be considered "voluntary," a company must disclose "all relevant facts known to it, including all relevant facts about the individuals involved in any FCPA violation." The Guidance cites to the Yates Memo as support for its requirement that companies disclose "facts related to involvement in the criminal activity by the corporation's officers, employees, or agents." Companies must also make officers and employees—including those located overseas—available for DOJ interviews (subject to the individuals' Fifth Amendment rights). In addition, to receive credit for "timely and appropriate remediation," companies must discipline employees responsible for the misconduct and implement "a system that provides for the possibility of disciplining others with oversight of the responsible individuals." Companies must also determine "how compensation is affected by both disciplinary infractions and failure to supervise adequately."

If a company fails to voluntarily disclose potential violations but otherwise fully cooperates and engages in timely and appropriate remediation of the misconduct, it will receive "at most a 25% reduction off the bottom of the Sentencing Guidelines fine range." In contrast, companies that meet all the rules outlined in the Guidance (voluntary disclosure, full cooperation, and remediation) will be eligible for "up to a 50% reduction off the bottom end of the Sentencing Guidelines fine range, if a fine is sought." Moreover, if at the time

---

[37] Department of Justice: Andrew Weissmann, "The Fraud Section's Foreign Corrupt Practices Act Enforcement Plan and Guidance" 5 Apr. 2016), *available at* https://www.justice.gov/opa/file/838386/download.

of resolution the company has implemented an effective compliance program, it will not be required to retain a corporate monitor. Under these circumstances, the DOJ may also consider a declination of prosecution.

Compliance Tips

Recent policy pronouncements and enforcement actions make clear that individuals face an increasing risk of liability under the FCPA. In an effort to reduce this risk, individuals should take steps to protect themselves from potential liability. Although no single step will fully insulate an individual from the DOJ, when taken together, these steps may help mitigate or even prevent FCPA violations.

1. **Embrace a culture of ethics and compliance.** Companies must develop and implement a robust anti-corruption compliance program. Not only does this mitigate risk for the company, but it also reduces the risk of liability for individuals. The compliance program should be tailored to risk, with the most resources and controls dedicated to the areas that create the greatest source of risk. Documenting adherence to the company compliance program will not only help prevent a potential violation of the law, but also provides individuals with a compelling argument should misconduct occur.

2. **Don't willfully ignore warning signs.** It is critical to conduct meaningful due diligence before entering into agreements with third parties or other business partners. Red flags must be investigated and, if they result in the discovery of potential wrongdoing, must be addressed. If company employees or third parties are suspected of paying bribes, this information must be reported to the company compliance officer and investigated. Ignoring red flags does not make them go away.

3. **It's not worth the risk.** When a high value transaction is on the line, individuals may be tempted to skirt FCPA compliance requirements in order to secure the deal. The risk is not worth the reward. Any improper payment, no matter how small, could jeopardize the reputation of an individual and the company. Moreover, once an individual begins down

this path, it is often difficult to stop. Corrupt officials rarely stop asking after they receive the first bribe—they return and often increase their demands. Although there are circumstances under which payments may need to be made (*i.e.*, when an individual's life or safety are threatened), these situations are rare and should be handled in accordance with a company's compliance program.

4. **Lead by example.** All employees play a critical role in defining the ethical culture of a company. Company management must be clear that bribery will never be tolerated, even if it results in the loss of business. A visible commitment to ethics and compliance is critical, as it sets the tone for the entire company. Employees (including senior executives) and board members should be trained regularly to ensure they understand the consequences of failing to comply with the FCPA and company compliance policies. And, when necessary, disciplinary action must be taken against employees that engage in wrongdoing—regardless of their position or value to the company.

5. **Don't be afraid to ask for help.** Individuals should be familiar with the best way to obtain guidance from the company on how to comply with the FCPA. The guidance should be viewed as a supplement, not a substitute, for training. Individuals should also have access to anonymous hotlines to enable them to obtain guidance in situations in which confidentiality is paramount.

Individuals must remain vigilant about their compliance with the FCPA. Understanding the reach of the FCPA is the first step in helping to mitigate or prevent potential violations under the statute.

Chapter 7
What You Should Know About the UK Bribery Act

The United Kingdom's Bribery Act of 2010 ("UKBA"), in force as of 1 July 2011, is a powerful piece of international legislation. But it is often treated as an afterthought to the similar law of its common-law cousin, the U.S. Foreign Corrupt Practices Act. This is understandable—the FCPA is, after all, the bread and butter of compliance professionals. But there are significant differences between the two laws that companies with a presence in or relation to the UK should be aware of.

The Provisions of the UKBA

First, a refresher on the black letter law—somewhat bitter, perhaps, like black tea, but it must be tasted before adding the FCPA to the brew. The black letter law is also significant because relatively few cases have been brought under the UKBA, so its provisions have not yet been the subject of significant appellate interpretation.

The UKBA establishes four types of crime. The first two attribute criminal liability to individuals, the other two to corporate entities.

Individual Liability for Bribery ("the simple offence")

At its core, the UKBA makes it a criminal offence for a person to offer, give, or promise a bribe.[1] A bribe is not confined to money, but is defined broadly as any financial or other advantage.[2] Bribery can be committed directly or through a third party,[3] and the bribe need

---

[1] UKBA s.1(2)(a) and 1(3)(a).

[2] UKBA s.1(2)(a) and 1(3)(a).

[3] UKBA s.1(5).

not actually be received by the person whom the briber intends to influence.[4]

Regarding state of mind, the UKBA requires one of two things. Either the briber must intend to induce a person to "perform improperly" a "relevant function or activity" (or to reward a person for such action); or the briber must know or believe that the recipient's acceptance of the bribe would itself constitute "improper performance" of a relevant function or activity.[5] Intention, knowledge, and belief are defined according to ordinary principles of law within the three jurisdictions of the UK.

A "relevant function" is defined as any function of a public nature,[6] while a "relevant activity" is an activity performed in connection with a business, in the course of employment, or on behalf of an incorporated or unincorporated body.[7] There is no requirement that a "relevant activity" be of a public nature, which means that the UKBA also criminalizes bribery in private business transactions. There is also no requirement that the function or activity take place in the UK or have any connection to the UK.[8] Relevant activities and functions also have a qualitative element: the person responsible for their performance (the intended recipient of the bribe) must to be expected to do so in good faith[9] or impartially,[10] or must occupy a position of trust by virtue of the activity or function.[11] "Improper performance" rests on the same qualitative element. If there is a breach of the expectation of good faith or impartiality either by an act or omission, that constitutes improper performance.[12]

This definition of improper performance as a breach of expectations (the "expectation test") raises the question of how enforcement agencies (and the courts) will interpret and define those expectations. The

---

[4] UKBA s.1(4).

[5] UKBA s.1(2)(b) & s.1(3)(b).

[6] UKBA s.3(2)(a).

[7] UKBA s.3(2)(b)–(d).

[8] UKBA s.3(6).

[9] UKBA s.3(3).

[10] UKBA s.3(4).

[11] UKBA s.3(5).

[12] UKBA s.4(1) & s.4(2)(a).

UKBA sets forth an objective standard: what a reasonable person in the UK would expect in relation to the performance of the activity or function. In doing so, it disregards any local custom or practice foreign to the UK.[13]

The UK-centric focus of the expectation test creates a potential disconnect with the actual expectations in the location where the performance takes place. For example, a briber intends to influence a South Korean businessman to perform a relevant function in Seoul and, as part of this, provides a low-value wedding gift and small offerings at every business meeting. Acceptance of such gifts may be entirely acceptable (indeed, a customary business courtesy) in the context of South Korean business culture. The same may not be not true according to the reasonable person in the UK, where the expectation of impartiality may require that such gifts not be offered. The relevant function comes under the UKBA despite occurring in South Korea, but is to be judged against the reasonable expectations of people in the UK.

The UKBA does provide a limited exception to the UK-centric expectation test where the performance of the activity or function is permitted or required by the written law of the foreign country or territory, but this only extends to written constitutions, applicable written legislation, and published judicial decisions.[14]

The briber's intention is directed to the quality of the recipient's performance, rather than to any material result. To commit this offence, there is no requirement that the briber intend to benefit from the bribery scheme by obtaining or retaining business or a business advantage. This is a significant difference from other offences within the UKBA (such as foreign public bribery and corporate liability for failure to prevent bribery) and similar legislation in other countries.

As well as addressing the supply-side of bribery by targeting bribers, the UKBA also targets individuals who receive bribes—the demand-side bribee.[15] The acts required for the demand-side offence match those of the supply-side, in that:

---

[13] UKBA s.5(1).

[14] UKBA s.5(3).

[15] UKBA s.2.

- A request for or agreement to receive a bribe is sufficient to constitute a bribe, in addition to actual acceptance of the bribe;[16]

- A bribe is defined broadly as a financial or other advantage;[17]

- A bribe can be either an incentive or a reward;[18]

- It is irrelevant whether the bribe is made through a third party, or for the benefit of a third party;[19]

- The same definitions of relevant activity, relevant function, improper performance, and the expectation test apply to the demand-side offence as they do to the supply-side offence;[20]

- The relevant activity or function need not take place in the UK nor have any connection to the UK.[21]

There are also similarities in the state-of-mind requirements. Specifically, a bribee can commit an offence by intending that, as a result of a bribe, a relevant function or activity should be performed improperly.[22] But in contrast to the supply-side offence, a bribee can also offend without having any specific intention, knowledge or belief. For example, the bribee is guilty of an offence where:

- The bribee requests, agrees to receive or accepts a bribe if the agreement, receipt or acceptance itself constitutes improper performance of a relevant activity or function irrespective of performing any additional activity or function;[23]

- The bribe is a reward for improper performance of a relevant activity or function;[24] or

---

[16] UKBA s.2(2)-s.2(5).

[17] UKBA s.2(2)-s.2(5).

[18] *Contrast* UKBA s.2(2) *and* s.2(3).

[19] UKBA s.2(2), s.2(4), s.2(5)(b) & s.2(6).

[20] UKBA s.3 & s.4–s.5.

[21] UKBA s.3(6).

[22] UKBA s.2(2).

[23] UKBA s.2(3).

[24] UKBA s.2(4).

- The anticipation or the consequence of the bribe results in improper performance of a relevant activity or function.[25]

When committed in any of these three ways, the offence requires no specific state of mind on the part of the bribee.

Jurisdiction to prosecute individuals for this type of offence under the UKBA in the UK courts rests on the familiar international-law concepts of territoriality and nationality. If any act or omission which forms part of the offence takes place in the UK, the UKBA provides jurisdiction to the UK courts irrespective of the nationality of the actors involved in bribery (both briber and bribee).[26] If no act or omission takes place in the UK, jurisdiction can nonetheless be asserted if the acts or omissions that occur abroad would have constituted the offence if they had occurred in the UK and, additionally, the defendant has "a close connection" to the UK.[27] That is, the briber or bribee must be a British citizen, British national, British subject, ordinarily reside in the UK, or fall into one of the more obscure categories of person which satisfy the close connection requirement.[28]

Individual Liability for Bribing a Foreign Public Official ("the foreign public official offence")

Foreign public official bribery is committed when a person bribes a foreign public official with the intent to influence the recipient in his or her public official capacity (by either act or omission) and to obtain or retain business or an advantage in the conduct of business.[29] As with the simple offence, the bribe may be any financial or other advantage, and liability extends to the offer and promise of a bribe as well as its actually delivery.[30] The offence may also be perpetrated through third parties.[31]

A foreign public official is an individual who either:

---

[25] UKBA s.2(5).

[26] UKBA s.12(1).

[27] UKBA s.12(2).

[28] UKBA s.12(4)(a)-(i).

[29] UKBA s.6(1) & s.6(2).

[30] UKBA s.6(3).

[31] UKBA s.6(3)(a).

- Occupies a legislative, administrative or judicial position of any kind in a country or territory outside the UK;[32]

- Exercises a public function on behalf of a country or territory outside the UK;[33]

- Exercises a public function on behalf of a public agency or public enterprise of a country or territory outside the UK;[34] or

- Is an official agent of a public international organisation.[35]

There is significant overlap between the simple offence of bribery and the foreign public official offence. A foreign public official, practically by definition, will perform a function of a public nature and, therefore, a "relevant function." A foreign public official is also likely to occupy a position of trust or be subject to an expectation of impartiality or good faith and, therefore, is likely to be performing a "relevant activity" within the meaning of the simple offence. Finally, simple-offence bribery need not be performed in the UK and so could include bribes intended to influence a foreign public official's actions abroad. This overlap is acknowledged in the UK Government's official guidance to the Act.[36]

There is, however, a significant difference between the two types of offence. In the foreign public official offence, the briber's intention is, in part, oriented toward the result rather than the performance—the foreign public official briber must *intend to obtain or retain business* or another advantage in the conduct of business. In addition, there is no requirement, as there is in the simple bribery offence, that the briber intend "improper performance" by the foreign official. All that is required in foreign official bribery is an intent to influence the foreign official in the performance of his or her function; such influence

---

[32] UKBA s.6(5)(a).

[33] UKBA s.6(5)(b).

[34] UKBA s.6(5)(b).

[35] UKBA s.5(c) & s.6(6).

[36] *See* "The Bribery Act 2010, Guidance about procedures which relevant commercial organisations can put into place to prevent persons associated with the from bribing" ("UKBA Guidance"), at 11.

need not be improper in the sense of violating any expectation of impartiality or good faith.

These differences were born out of a concern about obtaining evidence of the legitimate functions of foreign officials abroad, and were designed to make foreign official bribery easier to prove in UK courts by not requiring the court to examine the legitimacy of the foreign public official's functions. As the UK Government's guidance on the UKBA explains, "the exact nature of the functions of persons regarded as foreign officials is often very difficult to ascertain with any accuracy, and the securing of evidence will often be reliant on the co-operation of the state any such officials serve. . . . [I]t is not the Government's intention to criminalise behaviour where no . . . mischief occurs, but merely to formulate the offence to take account of [these] evidential difficulties".[37]

Despite these differences, there remains significant overlap between foreign public official bribery and the simple offence, allowing prosecutors discretion to decide which to pursue in any given case. These similarities include prosecutorial jurisdiction. If any act or omission which forms part of the offence takes place in the UK, the UKBA employs the territorial principle to afford jurisdiction to the UK courts.[38] If all acts or omissions take place outside the UK, jurisdiction exists if those acts or omissions would have formed part of the offence if they had occurred in the UK and the alleged briber has the requisite close connection to the UK.[39]

Corporate Criminal Liability for the Simple Offence and the Foreign Public Official Offence ("identification principle corporate liability")

Corporate entities can be held liable for the actions of certain individuals who bribe another person, are the recipient of a bribe, or bribe a foreign public official. The Act follows the traditional UK model of attributing criminal liability to corporations only through the words and actions of a small group of people who make up the

---

[37] *Id.*

[38] UKBA s.12(1).

[39] UKBA s.12(4)(a)-(i).

controlling mind or will of the organisation.[40] As the General Counsel to the Serious Fraud Office explains:

> [The] law in England and Wales is based on the idea that a company can only be convicted for the criminality of those who speak and act for the company. Those people, in turn, are made up of the company's leadership—conventionally understood to mean its directors as opposed to its rank and file employees . . . . We call this law the identification principle.
>
> The Bribery Act 2010 left the identification principle undisturbed. It follows that, if the evidence implicates a sufficiently senior person within the company, it can be held criminally liable for offences of bribery or bribery of foreign public officials.[41]

To implicate a company, the bribery must involve a director, manager, company secretary or similarly senior officer of the company, or someone purporting to act in such a capacity.[42] It is not necessary that the senior official directly commit the offence, but merely that he or she consent or connive in the commission of the bribery.[43] Both the senior officer and the company may be prosecuted where such consent or connivance is present.[44]

This type of corporate liability has one important limiting factor, contained in the Act's jurisdictional provisions: for criminal liability to attach to a corporation, the senior official who commits, consents to, or connives in the bribery must have a "close connection" with the UK.[45] Again, that means that the senior official must be a British citizen, British national, British subject, ordinarily reside in the UK,

---

[40] *See, e.g.*, similar provisions pursuant to s.18 of the Theft Act 1968, and s.12 of the Fraud Act.

[41] Speech of Alun Milford, General Counsel to the Serious Fraud Office, at the Handelsbatt Conference (14 Sept. 2016), *available at* https://www.sfo.gov.uk/2016/09/14/deferred-prosecution-agreements-perspective-england-wales/.

[42] UKBA s.14(4).

[43] UKBA s.14(2).

[44] UKBA s.14(2).

[45] UKBA s.14(2).

or fall into one of the more obscure close-connection categories.[46] In addition, because this type of liability is derivative of offences committed by individuals, the same territorial or nationality jurisdictional elements apply.[47]

Corporate Liability for Failure to Prevent Bribery ("the failure-to-prevent offence")

The UKBA makes it an offence for commercial organisations to fail to prevent bribery.[48] Given the traditional limitations under UK law on making companies criminally liable for the acts of their rank and file employees, and given the "close connection" of senior officials required for the first type of corporate liability, the scope of this final type of offence under the UKBA is significantly more expansive.

A "relevant commercial organisation" is guilty where a person associated with it bribes another person with the intent to obtain or retain business or a business advantage for the organisation.[49] Of immediate note is that while the Act criminalises the omissions or inadequacies of the company, it also requires an act on the part of the person associated with that company, namely a bribe. 'Bribe' has the same meaning as in the other bribery offences under the Act—both for bribing another person and for bribing a foreign public official.[50] But it is not necessary that a prosecution actually be brought or a conviction obtained against the briber for the company to be guilty of the failure-to-prevent offence.[51]

Here, the nature of the briber's association with the company can be significantly more attenuated than is required under the identification principle seen in the other type of corporate liability. To be associated with a company, a person need only perform services on its behalf.[52] This presumptively includes all of the company's em-

---

[46] UKBA s.12(4)(a)-(i).

[47] UKBA s.14.

[48] UKBA s.7.

[49] UKBA s.7(1).

[50] UKBA s.7(3).

[51] UKBA s.7(3)(a).

[52] UKBA s.8(1).

ployees,[53] as well as agents and subsidiaries.[54] But specific labels are not determinative; the central issue of whether the briber performs services on behalf of the company is ultimately a factual one, to be judged on all relevant circumstances as they appear to the jury, not simply the nature of the relationship between the briber and the company.[55]

Unlike the restricted "senior official" definition elsewhere in the Act, there is no requirement here that the briber associated with the company have a close connection to the UK. The briber could therefore be of any nationality and operating anywhere in the world. Similarly, the bribe itself need not occur in the UK—or indeed have any connection to the UK—for a company to be liable for failure-to-prevent.[56] The main limiting jurisdictional factor is the requirement that the company be a "relevant commercial organisation"—a term incorporating certain territorial elements. Specifically, a company is a relevant commercial organisation if it is either incorporated under UK laws or, alternatively, carries on any part of its business in the UK.[57]

An absolute defense is available where a defendant company can prove it had in place "adequate procedures designed to prevent persons associated with [the company] from undertaking such conduct."[58] Given the broad scope of the offense, the contours of this defense—and specifically what constitutes "adequate"—are likely to be of the utmost concern. The Act requires the Secretary of State for Justice to provide written guidance regarding what procedures should be put in place.[59] That guidance (first published in March 2011) is presented as a set of six non-prescriptive guiding principles of general application for creating and maintaining adequate procedures to prevent bribery:[60]

---

[53] UKBA s.8(3) and s.8(5).

[54] UKBA s.8(3).

[55] UKBA s.8(4).

[56] UKBA s.7(3), s.12(2)(a)-(b), s.12(3); *confirmed in* s.12(5)-(6).

[57] UKBA s.7(5).

[58] UKBA s.7(2).

[59] UKBA s.9(1).

[60] UKBA Guidance, at 6–7.

1. Proportionality – A company's procedures to prevent brib-
    ery should be proportionate to the risks it faces and to the
    nature, scale and complexity of the company's activities.[61]

2. Top-level commitment – A company's top-level manage-
    ment should be committed to preventing bribery by persons
    associated with the company, fostering a culture within the
    organisation in which bribery is never acceptable.[62]

3. Risk Assessment – The company should assess the nature
    and extent of its exposure to potential internal and ex-
    ternal risks of bribery on its behalf by persons associated
    with it. Such assessment should be periodic, informed and
    documented.[63]

4. Due Diligence – The company should apply proportionate
    risk-based due diligence procedures regarding persons who
    perform or will perform services on its behalf in order to
    mitigate identified bribery risks.[64]

5. Communication and Training – The company should en-
    sure that its bribery prevention policies and procedures
    are embedded and understood throughout the organisa-
    tion by means of internal and external communication and
    training.[65]

6. Monitoring and Review – The company should monitor
    and review its bribery-prevention procedures and make im-
    provements where needed.[66]

Although these principles are described as "outcome focussed,"[67] the
Secretary's guidance document acknowledges that "[n]o policies or
procedures are capable of detecting and preventing all bribery."[68]

---

[61] *Id.* at 21–22.

[62] *Id.* at 23–24.

[63] *Id.* at 25–26.

[64] *Id.* at 27–28.

[65] *Id.* at 29–30.

[66] *Id.* at 31.

[67] *Id.* at 20.

[68] *Id.* at 7.

Key Differences Between the UKBA and the FCPA

Having reviewed and compared the various offences set forth by the UKBA, we will now explore how the UKBA differs from the FCPA. A clear idea of the differences between the two legislative regimes can help expose gaps in anti-bribery procedures that are only based on a single piece of legislation.

Private Bribery

The most obvious distinction between the UKBA and the FCPA is that the UKBA covers private sector bribery. That coverage is not unlimited: because private bribery falls under the "simple offence" provision, it requires an intention that the bribe's recipient will perform a relevant activity improperly. As outlined previously, under the definition of "relevant activity" and the expectation test for improper performance, the bribee must be in a position of trust or one requiring the exercise of impartiality or good faith. Paying bribes to influence private sector functions or activities that do not entail such performance expectations would not constitute a crime under the UKBA.

It would be wrong to suggest that U.S. legislation completely ignores the issue of private bribery. Although not part of the FCPA, the Travel Act has the potential to federalize state legislation prohibiting private bribery, giving enforcement power to the federal courts. Still, although the distinction between the two countries' legislation is not as neat as it may first appear, it remains the case that the UKBA covers private bribery to a much greater extent than the FCPA.

Recipient of the Bribe

Unlike the FCPA, the UKBA criminalizes the demand-side of bribery transactions, targeting the bribee in addition to the briber. Again, this is accomplished under the provisions of the simple offence, rather than through the specific foreign public official offence.

There are limits to the extent a foreign public official can be prosecuted in the UK courts for receiving a bribe under the simple offence. For one thing, there is the concern expressed in the UK Government's guidance to the UKBA: that the functions of a foreign public official may be difficult to ascertain with any certainty, and would require cooperation from the other state to secure the relevant evidence.[69] There are also limits based on public international law as incorporated by UK domestic law, including immunity for certain public officials as well as the procedural requirements of extradition, given that UK criminal courts conduct trials in the absence of a defendant only in extremely limited circumstances.

Another limitation is jurisdictional. For the UK courts to have jurisdiction to prosecute the UKBA's simple offence, the act or omission forming part of the offence must take place in the UK, or the defendant (in this case the foreign public official) must have a "close connection" to the UK. Since there will only be very limited circumstances where a foreign public official will have the requisite close connection to the UK (for example dual citizenship, or residency in the UK), jurisdiction will more commonly turn on whether any part of the offence was committed in the UK.

So although the UKBA in principle allows the prosecution in UK courts of foreign officials who are recipients of bribes, such prosecutions have significant legislative and practical limitations and may only be pursued under the simple offence, not the specific foreign public official offence.

Definition of Public Official

The definition of a foreign public official under the UKBA differs from similar provisions under the FCPA. As outlined above, the UKBA defines foreign public official as including those who occupy a legislative, administrative or judicial position outside the UK; those who exercise a public function of behalf of a country, territory, public agency or public enterprise outside the UK; or an official agent of a public international organisation.[70] In contrast, the FCPA defines foreign official as:

> [A]ny officer or employee of a foreign government or any department, agency, or instrumentality thereof, or of any public international organization, or any person acting in an official capacity for or on behalf of any such government or department,

---

[69] *See supra*, note 37.

[70] UKBA s.6(5) and s.6(6).

agency, or instrumentality, or for or on behalf of any such public international organization.[71]

As noted elsewhere in this volume,[72] the U.S. Court of Appeals for the Eleventh Circuit has interpreted "instrumentality" in the above definition as "an entity controlled by the government of a foreign country that performs a function the controlling government treats as its own."[73] The UKBA, in contrast, focuses only on the position occupied by the official and the exercise of a public function. It does not necessarily require the same element of governmental control as is envisaged by the FCPA.

It is also noteworthy that while the FCPA criminalizes bribery of foreign political parties and candidates, the UKBA does not treat party officials or candidates as "public officials."

Intent Requirement for the Foreign Public Official Bribery Offence

Comparing the UKBA's foreign public official bribery offence with the FCPA prohibitions, the intent required of the perpetrator is not alike. The UKBA foreign public official offence requires only that the perpetrator intend to influence the foreign official in his or her public official capacity to obtain or retain business or an advantage in the conduct of business. The FCPA includes an additional qualitative element to the briber's intent in that the defendant must act "corruptly" as well as intend to obtain or retain business.

The FCPA, unlike the UKBA, also includes as one means of committing foreign public bribery the intention to secure an "improper" advantage—a qualitative element to the perpetrator's intent that is absent in the foreign public official offence under the UKBA. Even where corporate liability for the foreign public official offence is alleged—requiring, under the identification principle, the consent or connivance of a senior official—the consent requirement concerns the acts that senior officials must commit to be deemed involved in the offence, not the quality of their intention. The qualitative element

---

[71] Section 30A(f)(1)(A) of the Exchange Act, 15 U.S.C. § 78dd-1(f)(1)(A); 15 U.S.C. §§ 78dd-2(h)(2)(A), 78dd-3(f)(2)(A).

[72] *See* "What You Should Know About Foreign Officials" on page 1.

[73] *United States v. Esquenazi*, 752 F.3d 912, 925 (11th Cir. 2014).

to the briber's intent that is evident on the face of the FCPA is absent from the UKBA.

Facilitation Payments

The FCPA includes an exception for "any facilitating or expediting payment . . . the purpose of which is to expedite or to secure the performance of a routine governmental action." There is no such exception for facilitation payments under the UKBA. The UK Government's guidance states: "As was the case under the old law, the Bribery Act does not (unlike US foreign bribery law) provide any exception for [small payments to facilitate routine government action]."[74]

Although the UKBA prohibits facilitation payments, UK prosecuting agencies initially showed reluctance to pursue such prosecutions. Even the current guidance characterises the eradication of facilitation payments as "a long term objective."[75] In addition, the Serious Fraud Office has stated that "[i]t would be wrong to say there is no flexibility [in relation to facilitation payments]," and points to prosecutorial discretion to decline to bring such cases where the payment is small.[76] While there are clear differences in the legislation, because of the wide prosecutorial discretion within the UK, the enforcement with respect to facilitation payments may be similar in practice.

The Foreign Written Law Exception

Perhaps for fear of intruding on foreign countries' sovereignty, both the UKBA and FCPA include provisions by which a defendant can avoid conviction if payments were lawful under the laws of the foreign country.

Under the UKBA, for a payment to qualify as a bribe, the recipient foreign official must be "neither permitted nor required by the written laws applicable to [him] to be influenced in [his] capacity as a foreign pubic official" by the payment.[77] Where the "applicable law"

---

[74] UKBA Guidance, at 18.

[75] *Id.*

[76] *See* https://www.sfo.gov.uk/publications/guidance-policy-and-protocols/bribery-act-guidance/.

[77] UKBA s.6(3)(b).

is the law of the foreign country of which the official is a representative, the law must be contained in a written constitution, provision of legislation, or published judicial decision.[78] The absence of any foreign law justification for the payment is an element of the offence which the prosecution has to prove beyond reasonable doubt. Since the prosecution bears this burden, considerations of foreign law will also be a material factor in considering whether to bring the case in the first place.

The FCPA also provides a foreign law justification for the defendant's payments to a foreign official where such payments were "lawful under the written laws and regulations of the foreign official's . . . country." With no reference made to judicial decisions as part of the foreign country's law or to the rules of an international organization, the FCPA differs from the UKBA with respect to what constitutes relevant foreign law. More significantly, the written foreign law provisions of the FCPA are formulated as an affirmative defence. Thus, the defendant bears the burden of proving the payment's lawfulness to avoid conviction. A U.S. prosecutor therefore need not consider the content of foreign written laws in deciding whether to launch a prosecution. The UK prosecutor, in contrast, should satisfy himself that there is no local law justification before bringing the case to court.

Reasonable Bona Fide Expenditure Defence

A second affirmative defence under the FCPA is for bona fide expenditure, such as travel and lodging expenses, incurred in relation to the promotion, demonstration or explanation of products or services or for performance of a contract. The UKBA includes no such exception, suggesting that such payments may be more susceptible to prosecution in the UK than in the U.S.

However, the UK Government's guidance presents a picture of such expenses (where reasonable) as entirely lawful and so not requiring a defence in the first place. Such payments are characterised as "an established and important part of doing business and it is not the intention of the Act to criminalise such behaviour".[79] The guidance

---

[78] UKBA s.6(7)(c).

[79] UKBA Guidance, at 12.

suggests that such payments would not constitute an offence under the UKBA's public official bribery offence provisions because there is a legitimate intention other than financial or other advantage. Therefore, if the motives for payment were on par with those outlined in the FCPA's affirmative defence, no crime would have been committed under the UKBA foreign public official offence. Defining bona fide expenditures in this way—simply as not amounting to any special case—there is still scope under the UKBA for prosecution of unreasonable gifts and hospitality payments where the true intention is to obtain a business or other advantage.

Enforcement of the UKBA

The UKBA has been subject to very limited enforcement in comparison with the FCPA. The Serious Fraud Office ("SFO"), one of the three prosecution agencies charged under the UKBA with bringing cases, disclosed in May 2016 that it had charged five individuals and two companies with offences under the Act.[80] Although the Crown Prosecution Service has also brought charges for UKBA offences, these tend to focus on domestic bribery of relatively low value, and are not thought to number more than twenty cases.

Part of the reason for such limited enforcement is that the UKBA is not retroactive; therefore the conduct must have occurred after July 1, 2011. Given that many bribery cases take time to be detected, investigated and prosecuted, the present enforcement rates are said by the SFO to be the thin end of the wedge.

The UKBA, and UK law more generally, also affords significant prosecutorial discretion, which helps explain why enforcement actions, particularly against companies, have been so limited. The Director of the SFO was famously quoted as stating: "The sort of bribery we would be investigating would not be tickets to Wimbledon or bottles of champagne. We are not the 'serious champagne office'".[81] Similar statements pointing to the selectiveness of prosecuting agencies in deciding which cases to bring to court (choosing only those cases

---

[80] SFO response to Freedom of Information Request No. FOI2016-060, *available at* https://www.sfo.gov.uk/publications/corporate-information/freedom-of-information/.

[81] *See* "SFO: 'We are not the Serious Champagne Office'", Compliance Week (2 Sept. 2012), *available at* https://www.complianceweek.com/blogs/enforcement-action/sfo-we-are-not-the-serious-champagne-office.

that are clearly in the public interest) have been reiterated by the SFO. For example, in May 2016 the Joint Head of Bribery and Corruption at the SFO said publicly:

> The SFO exists to tackle the most serious or complex cases of fraud, bribery and corruption .... [W]hat this means in practice is that we will look carefully to determine whether any particular case is one that ought to be investigated by the SFO; that is to say, is the alleged offence likely to have a significant impact upon the UK's reputation as a safe place to do business; would the investigation require the use of the SFO's particular powers and operating model and is the scale or nature of the alleged offence such that there is a significant public interest to be met by commencing an investigation? If the answer to any of these questions is positive, then it is likely that the case is one that we would want to investigate.[82]

One element of enforcement practice that the SFO appears keen to make full use of is its ability to enter into Deferred Prosecution Agreements ("DPAs"). Two such agreements have been concluded following legislative amendments in 2013 which permitted this practice in the UK.[83] The legislation and guidance issued by prosecuting agencies sets out the following procedures:

1. To enter into a deferred prosecution agreement, the prosecuting agency still needs to bring the charges (and, therefore, be satisfied there is sufficient evidence and that it is in the public interest to prosecute).

2. Thereafter, the prosecutor has discretion as to whether to invite the defendant to enter into a deferred prosecution agreement. Informal statements by the SFO indicate that important considerations include "whether the company has cooperated with the SFO by shortening the process of the investigation and assisted in cases against the individuals

---

[82] Speech by Matthew Wagstaff, Joint Head of Bribery & Corruption, Serious Fraud Office, "The role and remit of the SFO" (18 May 2016).

[83] The Crimes and Court Act 2013, s.45 & Schedule 17.

who were responsible for the corrupt conduct."[84] Such cooperation will generally also include the company cooperating with any overseas investigations and prosecutions by foreign enforcement agencies.

3. Once the prosecution and defence have reached a written accord on the terms, the disposal by way of a DPA needs to be approved by a judge. Typically, the defendant will be required to disgorge profits, pay financial penalties and, on occasion, reimburse the costs of bringing the case.

4. There follows a period of time (usually three to five years) in which the agreement remains in force and the indictment is suspended to ensure compliance.

5. Following the completion of the DPA, the prosecuting agency applies to the court to dismiss the charges and the proceedings are concluded.

Although enforcement of the UKBA has so far been relatively modest, some of the cases have resulted in significant sums being paid. For example, the case against Standard Bank (one of the DPAs and the first prosecution for the failure to prevent bribery offence) resulted in the payment of a settlement figure of USD 25.2 million.

Practical Considerations of the UKBA for Companies' Compliance Processes

The UKBA and FCPA differ in important respects in terms of scope, application and enforcement. In order to limit liability under the UKBA, a company should:

1. Determine whether it, its subsidiaries, or anyone doing business on its behalf is incorporated according to the laws of any jurisdiction within the UK, or does any part of its business within the UK;

---

[84] Alun Milford, General Counsel of the SFO "Deferred Prosecution Agreements – the perspective from England and Wales" (14 Sept. 2016), *available at* https://www.sfo.gov. uk/2016/09/14/deferred-prosecution-agreements-perspective-england-wales/.

2. Determine whether the company's compliance procedures cover private bribery;

3. Determine whether the company's compliance procedures cover bribe recipients;

4. Incorporate the six guiding principles of effective compliance regimes, as outlined in the UK Government's non-binding guidance, to limit liability for the failure to prevent bribery offence;

5. Be aware that corporate liability may attach to the basic bribery offences of bribing and being bribed when committed by senior company officials with a close connection to the UK; and

6. Carefully monitor and train senior officials within the company, particularly those with a close connection to the UK.

Chapter 8
What You Should Know About Cost-Effective Compliance

Anti-bribery compliance costs are rising. In 2016 alone, U.S. foreign bribery–related settlements between the private sector and the DOJ and the SEC resulted in an average penalty per company of approximately USD 75 million. Despite the large size of these penalties, companies embroiled in enforcement actions routinely conclude that the fines they pay are in fact less expensive than the costs of the in¬vestigations and remediation. Even for a company not in the middle of an ongoing investigation, there is an expectation that the company should be doing everything it can to prevent bribery from occurring within the organization. Indeed, many anti-bribery laws penalize companies for inadequate compliance procedures even in the absence of any bribery.

At the same time, many compliance officers express frustration that their programs are expected, year upon year, to be more sophisticated and broader in reach—without raising costs to do so. But although there is a limit to how far travel, training, due diligence, and risk-assessment budgets can be stretched, there is some good news for corporate compliance officers: government organizations, civil society, and the philanthropic arms of some institutions have been working to develop online compliance tools that are available to use at little or no cost.

In this chapter, we offer a survey of these free-of-cost and low-cost compliance resources in an effort to assist compliance officers with designing and implementing anti-bribery compliance programs at their companies. Of course, even the sum total of all of these resources will never be able to constitute the entirety of a company's compliance program, which will differ for each company. But by leveraging these tools and resources, in-house counsel can begin to address many key issues while reallocating resources to other critical areas of compliance.

Informational Resources

Standards and Guidance

Many government agencies responsible for enforcing anti-bribery laws have published guidelines and policy protocols meant to help companies understand how those agencies interpret and enforce the law. These guidelines seek to provide clarity not only for companies under investigation, but also for companies wishing to build defensible compliance programs. Two of the most well-known guidelines have been published by the U.S. and UK authorities:

- **A Resource Guide to the U.S. Foreign Corrupt Practices Act.**[1] Released in November 2012, this guide was the result of a joint collaboration between the DOJ and SEC to provide clarity regarding the provisions of the FCPA and its enforcement. The guide addresses a wide variety of topics, ranging from the definition of a "foreign official" under the FCPA to how successor liability applies in the mergers and acquisitions context. It also covers the hallmarks of an effective corporate compliance program, providing a general overview of those aspects that the DOJ and SEC assess when evaluating a program's strength.

- **The UK Bribery Act 2010 Guidance.**[2] Published in 2011 by the United Kingdom's Serious Fraud Office ("SFO"), this guide covers adequate procedures, facilitation payments, and business expenditures under the UK Bribery Act 2010. The UK government has also published rules governing the application and approval process for deferred prosecution agreements ("DPAs")[3] as well as guidance regarding corporate self-reporting.[4]

---

[1] https://www.justice.gov/sites/default/files/criminal-fraud/legacy/2015/01/16/guide.pdf

[2] https://www.justice.gov/sites/default/files/criminal-fraud/legacy/2015/01/16/guide.pdf

[3] http://www.justice.gov.uk/courts/procedure-rules/criminal/docs/2012/guide-to-criminal-procedure-amendment-no-2-rules-2013.pdf

[4] https://www.sfo.gov.uk/publications/guidance-policy-and-protocols/corporate-self-reporting/

The DOJ has also issued an eight-page guidance document on "Evaluation of Corporate Compliance Programs,"[5] offering a condensed summary of "some important topics and sample questions that the Fraud Section has frequently found relevant in evaluating a corporate compliance program."

In addition to these enforcement agency guidelines, numerous intergovernmental organizations and NGOs have published policy documents to provide corporate compliance officers with a top-down view of enforcement trends and techniques. One of the most comprehensive of these is the **Anti-Corruption Ethics and Compliance Handbook,**[6] a collaborative effort by the Organisation for Economic Co-operation and Development ("OECD"), the United Nations Office on Drugs and Crime ("UNODC"), and the World Bank. The handbook covers risk assessments, support and commitment from senior management, policies, internal controls, recordkeeping, and promoting and incentivizing ethics and compliance within the organization. Other anti-bribery guidelines for businesses include the following:

- Corporate Governance and Business Integrity: A Stocktaking of Corporate Practices (OECD 2015);[7]

- Guide to Corporate Sustainability (UN Global Compact 2015);[8]

- APEC General Elements of Effective Voluntary Corporate Compliance Programs (Asia-Pacific Economic Cooperation 2014);[9]

- Business Principles for Countering Bribery (Transparency International 2013);[10]

---

[5] https://www.justice.gov/criminal-fraud/page/file/937501/download.

[6] https://www.unodc.org/documents/corruption/Publications/2013/Anti-CorruptionEthics-ComplianceHandbook.pdf

[7] http://www.oecd.org/corruption/corporate-governance-business-integrity-stocktaking-corporate-practices.htm

[8] https://www.unglobalcompact.org/docs/publications/UN_Global_Compact_Guide_to_Corporate_Sustainability.pdf

[9] http://mddb.apec.org/Documents/2014/SOM/CSOM/14_csom_041.pdf

[10] http://www.transparency.org/whatwedo/publication/business_principles_for_countering_bribery

- An Anti-Corruption Ethics and Compliance Programme for Business: A Practical Guide (UNODC 2013);[11]

- ICC Rules on Combating Corruption (International Chamber of Commerce 2011);[12]

- Business Against Corruption: A Framework For Action (UN Global Compact 2011);[13]

- Summary of World Bank Group Integrity Compliance Guidelines (World Bank 2010);[14]

- Good Practice Guidance on Internal Controls, Ethics, and Compliance (OECD 2010);[15]

- Partnering Against Corruption — Principles for Countering Bribery (World Economic Forum 2009);[16] and

- APEC Anti-corruption Code of Conduct for Business (Asia-Pacific Economic Cooperation 2007).[17]

In addition, the International Organization for Standardization has established the **ISO 37001** standard for **anti-bribery management systems**,[18] presented both as an aid to the implementation of corporate anti-bribery compliance programs and as a reference point for certifying auditors. The ISO 37001 standards and guidance (which can be purchased online) are generic and largely reflect best practices already established by the international community in the above-mentioned guidelines. Even so, ISO 37001 articulates familiar principles from the perspective of a neutral, non-governmental international organization, not bound to the authority of any particular jurisdiction.

---

[11] http://www.unodc.org/documents/corruption/Publications/2013/13-84498_Ebook.pdf

[12] https://iccwbo.org/publication/icc-rules-on-combating-corruption/

[13] https://www.unglobalcompact.org/docs/news_events/8.1/bac_fin.pdf

[14] http://siteresources.worldbank.org/INTDOII/Resources/Integrity_Compliance_Guidelines.pdf

[15] http://www.oecd.org/daf/anti-bribery/44884389.pdf

[16] http://www3.weforum.org/docs/WEF_PACI_Principles_2009.pdf

[17] http://publications.apec.org/publication-detail.php?pub_id=269

[18] http://www.iso.org/iso/home/store/catalogue_tc/catalogue_detail.htm?csnumber=65034

Anti-Corruption Databases

Every year, companies avoid protracted litigation by settling with enforcement agencies regarding corruption-related activities. Given how rarely such cases go to trial, these settlement agreements make up the bulk of anti-bribery case law, and can provide key insights as to what constitutes bribery and how company compliance programs fail to detect and prevent wrongdoing. The TRACE **Compendium of Anti-Bribery Cases**[19] provides detailed information on all transnational anti-bribery cases and most investigations in a fully searchable format. For example, it's possible to search for cases involving China, gifts and hospitality, and the communications industry. The compendium's scope is also far broader than just FCPA cases. As long as the matter crosses an international border, it's in the compendium. TRACE generally updates the compendium within 24 hours of news of any developments. Users can register to receive a brief "alert" whenever a significant matter is added or updated.

In addition, data from the TRACE compendium is collated annually in the **TRACE Global Enforcement Report**,[20] showing trends over time, by country and by industry, with every data point supported by a full description of each matter in the compendium.

For those solely interested in researching FCPA-related material, it may be worthwhile to have a look at the **Foreign Corrupt Practices Act Clearinghouse**,[21] a joint collaboration between Stanford University's Rock Center for Corporate Governance and the law firm of Sullivan & Cromwell LLP. The clearinghouse serves as a repository of original source documents, providing users with detailed information relating to enforcement of the FCPA.

Other databases collect laws and regulations relevant to jurisprudence in other parts of the world. The UNODC, for example, has launched a web-based anti-corruption portal known as **TRACK (Tools and Resources for Anti-Corruption Knowledge)**,[22] which features a legal library on the United Nations Convention against

---

[19] http://traceinternational.org/compendium

[20] http://traceinternational.org/publications

[21] http://fcpa.stanford.edu/index.html

[22] http://www.track.unodc.org/Pages/home.aspx

Corruption ("UNCAC"), including laws from over 175 States organized by the requirements of the convention they implement.

Several think tanks have created more general resource centers, collecting papers and other public source material aimed at provoking thought in the area of combating corruption. The **U4 Anti-Corruption Resource Centre**,[23] an initiative of the ministers of international development from Australia, Denmark, Finland, Germany, Norway, Switzerland, Sweden and the UK, includes publications on themes ranging from international drivers of corruption, to corruption in the aid sector and natural resource management. Finally, the **World Bank Virtual Resource Center on Business Ethics and Anti-Corruption**[24] includes links to works on drafting codes of conduct, case studies, videos and presentations, as well as more general resources.

There are also several universities that have public, online web portals where it's possible to find the latest academic research on bribery- and corruption-related topics, as well as calendars for live events and speakers:

- Columbia Law School's Center for the Advancement of Public Integrity;[25]

- The Rutgers Institute on Anti-Corruption Studies;[26]

- Harvard University's Edmond J. Safra Center for Ethics;[27]

- The Oxford Centre for the Study of Corruption and Transparency;[28]

- The Sussex Centre for the Study of Corruption;[29]

- Griffith University's Institute for Ethics, Governance and Law;[30]

---

[23] http://www.u4.no/

[24] http://go.worldbank.org/1ADEO3UGS0

[25] http://web.law.columbia.edu/public-integrity

[26] https://riacs.newark.rutgers.edu/about

[27] http://ethics.harvard.edu/

[28] https://podcasts.ox.ac.uk/series/oxford-centre-study-corruption-and-transparency

[29] http://www.sussex.ac.uk/scsc/

[30] https://www.griffith.edu.au/criminology-law/institute-ethics-governance-law

- The Wharton School's Carol and Lawrence Zicklin Center for BusinessEthics Research;[31]

- University College London's Centre for Ethics and Law;[32] and

- Richmond School of Law's International Bribery Scholarship Database;[33]

In addition, Transparency International's **Anti-Corruption Research Network (ACRN)**[34] offers an online platform for anti-corruption academic researchers to share findings and exchange ideas and information with their peers in the academic field as well as with practitioners.

Country and Industry Resources

There are several tools available to aid compliance officers in assessing geographic risk for corruption. The **TRACE Matrix**[35] provides a specific measure of business bribery risk in nearly two-hundred countries across four domains: (i) business interactions with government, (ii) anti-bribery laws and enforcement, (iii) government and civil service transparency, and (iv) the capacity for civil society oversight. Nine subdomains further break down the risk indicators resulting in a total of fourteen scores. Companies can use this information not only to identify particularly challenging areas, but also to implement appropriate risk-mitigation measures. For example, in a country with a high score in domain 1 (business interactions with government) a company may consider building more time into projects to get through red tape lawfully, as tight deadlines in countries with high levels of bribery make companies easy targets for bribe demands.

Transparency International's annual **Corruption Perceptions Index**[36] offers a more general look at perceived corruption risks, using

---

[31] http://www.zicklincenter.org/

[32] http://www.ucl.ac.uk/laws/law-ethics

[33] http://law.richmond.libguides.com/c.php?g=129551&p=846446

[34] http://corruptionresearchnetwork.org/

[35] http://traceinternational.org/trace-matrix

[36] http://www.transparency.org/research/cpi/

12 different data sources from 11 institutions that capture perceptions of corruption within the past two years, which are then aggregated and standardized on a scale of 0–100. Transparency International also publishes the **Global Corruption Barometer**,[37] which surveys a sampling of people worldwide to capture attitudes towards corruption.

Also of note is the Basel Institute on Governance's **B20 Collective Action Hub**,[38] which offers a global map and list of anti-corruption collective action initiatives by country. The Institute has also developed an **Anti–Money Laundering Index**,[39] which aggregates third party data from sources such as the FATF, the World Bank, and the World Economic Forum to rank countries by their risk of money laundering and terrorist financing.

For those interested in industry-specific information, there are several organizations that provide anti-bribery resources aimed at specific sectors. The **Global Infrastructure Anti-Corruption Centre (GIACC)**,[40] for example, is an independent not-for-profit organization which provides resources to assist in the understanding, identification and prevention of corruption in the infrastructure, construction and engineering sectors. Another sector-specific resource is **Ethicana**,[41] a 42-minute training video about corruption in the global construction industry made available to the public free of charge by the Anti-Corruption Education and Training Initiative, a consortium of agencies including the American Society of Civil Engineers. There are similar anti-bribery initiatives with respect to the following industries:

- Defense;[42]

- International development;[43]

---

[37] http://www.transparency.org/research/gcb/

[38] http://www.collective-action.com/initiatives/map

[39] https://index.baselgovernance.org/

[40] http://www.giaccentre.org/

[41] http://www.ethicana.org/

[42] http://government.defenceindex.org/

[43] http://guide.iacrc.org/

- Extractives;[44]

- Maritime;[45] and

- Pharmaceuticals and healthcare.[46]

While many of the tools and resources found in these online portals are intended for a particular industry audience, they also provide general information that can be applied to other sectors as well.

News Sources

One of the most difficult tasks for a compliance officer is keeping abreast of new developments in the field. Fortunately, there are many very good anti-bribery blogs and email alerts, dense with information and updated several times each week. While judicious assessment of such sources may at times be warranted, sophisticated readers can nevertheless learn much from these authors' hard work and benefit from having succinct updates delivered to their inboxes on a daily basis.

One of the more objective news sources is **TrustLaw**,[47] an online center for anti-corruption news, run by the Thomson Reuters Foundation, the charitable arm of Thomson Reuters. For those who subscribe to the Wall Street Journal, its **Risk & Compliance Journal**[48] is also an excellent news source.

In addition, the **FCPA Blog**,[49] maintained by Richard Cassin, provides a wealth of timely, sane analyses of the latest anti-bribery news. There are dozens of others, so you might want to consider using an RSS feed reader to help curate your news.

---

[44] http://www.resourcegovernance.org/

[45] http://www.maritime-acn.org/

[46] http://ti-health.org/

[47] http://www.trust.org/trustlaw/

[48] http://blogs.wsj.com/riskandcompliance/

[49] http://www.FCPAblog.com/

Policies and Procedures

Benchmarking anti-bribery programs is a good way for companies to keep themselves well within the compliance pack, but many are reluctant to start the conversa¬tion. The UNODC, with the support of the Swedish government and the accounting firm PricewaterhouseCoopers, has collected the anti-bribery programs of the **Fortune 500 Global Index (2008)**[50] and made them publicly available. In addition, the Illinois Institute of Technology's Center for the Study of Ethics in the Professions maintains an online collection of over 1,000 Codes of Ethics in one place.[51]

There are also organizations, like the International Chamber of Commerce ("ICC"), that have published model policies and guides on topics like gifts and hospitality[52] and third party due diligence.[53] The ICC also has released a model **Anti-corruption Clause**,[54] which can be used in third-party contracts. The U.S. Department of State,[55] the UK government,[56] the United Nations and World Health Organization,[57] and the European Union[58] all publicly disclose their own per diem thresholds for almost all cities, broken down by meals, accommodation, and incidentals, which can be useful in benchmarking similar policies in-house.

Training

An increasingly scattered workforce means that in-person anti-bribery training is not always a viable option. Online training tools are popular with compliance professionals because they are easy to administer, multi-lingual, and auditable. Online training is, of course,

---

[50] http://www.unodc.org/unodc/en/corruption/anti-corruption-policies-and-measures-of-the-fortune-global-500.html

[51] http://ethics.iit.edu/ecodes/introduction

[52] https://iccwbo.org/publication/icc-guidelines-on-gifts-and-hospitality/

[53] https://iccwbo.org/publication/icc-anti-corruption-third-party-due-diligence/

[54] https://iccwbo.org/publication/icc-anti-corruption-clause/

[55] https://aoprals.state.gov/content.asp?content_id=184&menu_id=78

[56] https://www.gov.uk/government/uploads/system/uploads/attachment_data/file/359797/2014_Worldwide_subsistence_rates.pdf

[57] http://apps.who.int/bfi/tsy/PerDiem.aspx

[58] https://ec.europa.eu/europeaid/sites/devco/files/perdiem-rate-20150318.pdf

not a perfect substitute for in-person training. Skills such as problem-solving and experiential learning—both of which are important facets of anti-bribery training—are best developed through in-person training, where the experience can be personalized on the spot by drawing out participants' concerns. But online training can serve as a useful and cost-effective supplement to a company's compliance program—if it is well-designed and well-presented, and ensures that employees are engaged and attentive.

TRACE offers a free one-hour-long training video entitled **Toxic Transactions: Bribery, Extortion and the High Price of Bad Business**.[59] The video, which was produced by NBC Universal's Peacock Productions, is a lively and informative anti-bribery training video designed for employees at all levels, featuring commentary from the DOJ, SEC, and FBI, as well as the UK's Serious Fraud Office, the OECD, and the World Bank. It's a great way to initiate the anti-corruption conversation with employees and a strong addition to the compliance officer's anti-bribery training toolkit.

There are also several free online courses available. In early 2016, the **UNODC Global eLearning Program**[60] launched two new modules: "Introduction to Anti-corruption" and "Advanced Anti-corruption: Prevention of Corruption." Both courses are primarily focused on the provisions of the United Nations Convention against Corruption ("UNCAC"). The UNODC and the UN Global Compact also offer a free online training tool called **The Fight Against Corruption**,[61] which covers topics such as gifts and hospitality, facilitation payments, intermediaries, and insider information. Other free online anti-bribery courses include a one-and-a-half hour long training entitled **Doing Business Without Bribery**[62] created by Transparency International, as well as a 30-minute course covering the basics of anti-bribery compliance offered by the **GAN Business Anti-Corruption Portal**.[63]

---

[59] https://www.youtube.com/playlist?list=PLyEfKIedJVVX9MWPW4iTLddkYXVf44sFf

[60] http://www.unodc.org/unodc/en/corruption/news-elearning-course.html

[61] http://thefightagainstcorruption.org/

[62] http://www.doingbusinesswithoutbribery.com/

[63] http://elearning.business-anti-corruption.com/

For those companies operating in Spanish-speaking parts of the world, another option is the **MOOC Chile Transparency and Anti-Corruption Course**,[64] which emphasizes transparency and anti-corruption practices in the public domain and includes case studies from Argentina, Brazil, Chile, Spain, Mexico, Peru and Venezuela. ("MOOC" is an acronym for "Massive Open Online Courses," and the program is funded by the Ford Foundation in New York.)

Otherwise, some of the best available resources are meant as supplements to and aids for live, in-person trainings. The ICC, working together with the United Nations Global Compact, Transparency International, and the World Economic Forum, has published a very helpful pamphlet called **RESIST: Resisting Extortion and Solicita¬tion in International Transactions**.[65] The authors are primarily in-house counsel, and, as the title suggests, they provide brief scenarios describing tips for resisting demands for bribes and extortionate payments. The UN Global Compact also offers an entire suite of anti-corruption tools, organized around 10 themes, entitled the **PRME Anti-Corruption Toolkit**.[66] The toolkit is primarily intended as a guide for the classroom, but it can equally be used by compliance officers for in-house trainings.

Learning about resisting bribery isn't just for your present-day workforce. In its 2016 "United Against Corruption" campaign, the UN emphasized the importance of engaging youth in understanding what corruption is and how to fight it.[67] In support of that goal, TRACE has developed **Bribe Busters**,[68] a series of short animated videos and comic books designed to teach children about bribery's effects on society and how they can stand up to it. Freely available in multiple languages, the series is an example of the kind of resource that can be used to extend anti-corruption efforts beyond your organization and into the broader community.

---

[64] http://mooc.udp.cl/transparency-and-anti-corruption/

[65] https://iccwbo.org/publication/resisting-extortion-and-solicitation-in-international-transactions-resist/

[66] http://actoolkit.unprme.org/modules/introduction/

[67] http://www.anticorruptionday.org/actagainstcorruption/en/about-the-campaign/what-can-you-do.html.

[68] https://www.traceinternational.org/bribe-busters.

Managing Third Party Relationships

Managing third party relationships often takes up a disproportionate share of a compliance officer's time and effort. Conducting due diligence on third parties is both time-consuming and expensive. That trend is unlikely to abate anytime soon as more companies move toward an overseas model of vertical disintegration which relies on a global supply chain to handle non-core manufacturing and service activities.

Fortunately for compliance officers, new models for doing due diligence are upending traditional methods and reducing costs. TRACE offers a "portable" certification model for due diligence which shifts the responsibility for vetting anti-bribery concerns to intermediaries who—once approved—maintain their own compliance information. TRACE stores all of these third party reports in its **Intermediary Directory**,[69] creating a publicly searchable database of vetted, sanctions-screened and trained small and medium-sized enterprises ("SMEs"). SMEs included in the Intermediary Directory have completed the comprehensive TRACE*certification* review and analysis process (or have renewed their certification within the last year) and have provided their consent to appear in the public list. The Intermediary Directory streamlines the process of identifying and contacting potential new business partners.

TRACE has also created the world's only global beneficial ownership register, called TRACE*public*.[70] Developed to encourage greater corporate transparency, the online database contains beneficial ownership information on thousands of companies in more than 100 countries. Users need only the name of a company or one owner to conduct a search. Like the Intermediary Directory, TRACE*public* is free to use and leverages a collective-action approach to due diligence in order to increase transparency around international standards.

That regulators and enforcement agencies expect more sophistication from corporate compliance programs does not necessarily mean that companies must spend more money on new tools and resources. When building out complete and robust compliance programs, in-house counsel should weigh all options, including free and low-cost

---

[69] https://tpms.traceinternational.org/IntermediaryDirectory

[70] https://tpms.traceinternational.org/TRACEpublic

offerings that exist. For the seasoned compliance officer, a dynamic and engaging compliance program is not the result of a single solution, but rather a melding of various components.

Chapter 9
Compliance Tips: Due Diligence Assessments

Due Diligence Assessments: The Cult of the Imperfect

In case the headline of this column already has made your compliance blood run cold, let me be clear: Due diligence on third parties should be as close to perfect as professionally possible, given an appropriate budget and the available tools. It is the risk assessment leading up to this due diligence that won't be perfect—because it can't be. A roomful of compliance officers will never agree on the precise criteria for a risk-ranking exercise, and they certainly won't agree on the relative weights to assign to each. The debate could last for years without leading to a useful conclusion.

Sir Robert Alexander Watson-Watt is credited with saving thousands of lives in Britain during the worst days of World War II after developing Chain Home, a low-frequency radar system able to detect aircraft from about 90 miles away. He openly encouraged what he called the "cult of the imperfect" among his team. He knew that Britain didn't need the best possible radar system in five years; the country needed a viable radar system urgently. *Immediately*. Watson-Watt, who was knighted shortly after the Battle of Britain, is said to have instructed his team to strive for the third-best option, because "the second-best comes too late . . . the best never comes."

I frequently speak with companies that are ready to launch an assessment of the risk associated with each category of their third-party intermediaries. We discuss appropriate indicators of risk: geography, government as opposed to commercial customers, fixed versus contingent compensation, deal size, etc. We develop and test the weighting of each criterion and determine whether the results generally reflect the company's understanding of their bribery risk, including risk associated with their industry.

And then, at times, the project stalls. The company concludes that, with more time, more research and more testing, they will reach a more perfect assessment of their risk and so be able to deploy the different levels of due diligence with greater precision. That may be true. But in the eight or 10 months that it takes to conduct that additional research and adjust the algorithm in subtle ways, they also might be able to collect ownership information from all third parties and screen it against international watch lists. Or they might be able to identify (approximately, imperfectly) their highest-risk partners and roll out their most rigorous level of due diligence for those, identifying ties to the government or significant past misconduct. There might even be time to require everyone in the top category to complete online antibribery training.

Launching a due diligence program can be unnerving. Many companies aren't confident that they know the total universe of their third parties. They're concerned about what they may find. They worry that their resources will be overstretched and their program will stall.

So how do you get an imperfect due diligence assessment going? Just get started. After making a reasonable effort to establish the scope of the project and a commonsense assessment of the levels of risk, dive in. You can reassess and adjust at intervals. In fact, you're encouraged to by most enforcement agencies. Tinkering with your approach to due diligence is a sign of an evolving, increasingly sophisticated program, not an admission of error.

If one of your third parties pays a bribe on your company's behalf six months from now, you'll still be better off having the riskiest 15 percent of your intermediaries, give or take a few percentage points, trained and vetted than a fourth iteration of an algorithm that was only ever meant to be a path to a goal, not the goal itself.

Perfect due diligence risk assessments never come. And even second-best may come too late. Just get started. You'll see more protections and benefits from good (for now) than *perfect* (some day, maybe ...)

Chapter 10
Compliance Tips: Due Diligence On Intermediaries

Difficult Due Diligence on Overseas Intermediaries

We all know how important it is to conduct meaningful due diligence on third-party intermediaries. While these parties can perform crucial functions for companies seeking to expand their worldwide presence—opening up new markets, providing access to decision-makers, helping to identify opportunities and trends—they can also subject companies to serious financial liability and reputational harm. As compliance officers know well, under the Foreign Corrupt Practices Act (FCPA), if the agent of a company pays or offers to pay a bribe to a foreign official in order to help the company secure business, the company itself can be held responsible, whether or not the company authorized or even knew about the bribe. Given the magnitude of the potential liability—settlements for FCPA violations can run into tens of millions of dollars—it is crucial to know something about the background of the person or entity that's being considering to represent the company abroad.

Sometimes, the information discovered through a due-diligence inquiry will be a clear deal-breaker—a prior bribery conviction, for example. Very rarely will the candidate will have the track record of a boy scout. But there is a vast middle ground. A potential intermediary's record may be not be spotless, but still may not be disqualifying. Consider the following scenarios:

- A criminal-record review shows that the sole owner of an entity you are considering to represent your company was convicted of drunk driving ten years ago.

The principal's drunk-driving conviction certainly affects her reputation, but does it make her more likely to pay a bribe? What if her representation of your company requires near-constant driving to meetings at which she'll represent your company? Does that exacerbate the problem? What about the fact that the conviction was ten years ago? Is that long enough to allow her a clear slate? Does it matter whether she was in her early 20s at the time? In her early 40s?

- A similar review shows that one of four equal partners in a potential intermediary was charged with assault five years ago. He is very well-connected and the charges were later dropped.

There is an obvious reputational issue here, along with possible questions about the partner's judgment. On the other hand, there was never any conviction. Are you expected to investigate allegations of misconduct that were made and dropped five years earlier? At the same time, in jurisdictions with questionable judicial systems, there may be questions about the reason the charges were dropped. If it was because of the partner's connections, does that give rise to worries about his willingness to game the system?

- A channel partner fighting to get your business tells you that your current partner is "widely known" to pay kickbacks to government officials.

This time, the allegations are directly on-point. They cannot be ignored. However, the competitor has no proof of misconduct and a very clear interest in discrediting the current partner. How far do you have to look for evidence that would support the competitor's claim, to "prove the negative"? Can you rest easy if you don't find anything, or do you need to take additional steps to assure yourself of the competitor's business practices?

- During a general tax amnesty in the Philippines last year, your sales representative came forward, admitted to five years of unpaid taxes, and paid the outstanding balance with interest and penalties.

Tax evasion is a significant red flag, and the misconduct here is both admitted and recent. The sales representative has corrected the misconduct, which is a positive sign, but what was her motive for doing so? Was she just taking advantage of the amnesty to assuage a fear of getting caught? Does it matter, or is it even possible to determine, whether she had a genuine change of heart? If one year in the past is too recent, how many additional years of impeccable conduct would be sufficient? Would it make any difference if the representative's situation was a common one? If, say, fully 70% of small businesses in the Philippines had taken advantage of the amnesty?

These scenarios all raise red flags, some more worrying than others. They are typical of the kinds of constant, low-grade issues that arise in the course of due diligence. Given the scale of the penalties involved if a company intermediary is involved in bribery, one might imagine adopting a policy under which any red flag is disqualifying. In some markets, though, you might find it difficult to find anyone you could approve under that sort of zero tolerance standard.

But how much is too much? None of the above scenarios provides a clear indication that the individual or entity in question is going to cause problems for your company. All a red flag tells you is that there could be a problem, and closer scrutiny might be warranted. No company can devote unlimited resources to such scrutiny. At some point, a decision has to be made.

You don't have unlimited time to make that decision, either. The world moves fast, and opportunities can be lost. A company's compliance team can be under significant pressure not to hold things up on the business end. On the one hand, you don't want to rush things when you believe there is genuine cause for concern. On the other hand, you don't want to unduly delay matters by fretting over things that may not matter all that much. At what point should you let yourself sign off on the engagement?

Here is something important to keep in mind: Although the process of conducting due diligence is somewhat mechanical, the process of acting on that due diligence should not be. Even if it were possible, say, to assign a point-value to each type of red flag that might arise, it would be unwise for a company to base its decisions regarding intermediaries solely on whether their total flag-points exceed a certain threshold. Such a system would not adequately take into account the context in which a given intermediary will be operating, and the ways in which the flagged circumstances may or may not be relevant in that context. You want to minimize the risk of non-compliant behavior by intermediaries, not just maximize the speed with which you make your approval decisions.

Of course, depending on the size of your company and its operations, you're probably not going to be able to personally conduct a full evaluation of each potential intermediary your company may engage. You can't get by without protocols and standards for review, reporting and escalation. Establishing and justifying such protocols can itself be a crucial element in showing enforcement agencies that your company has a well-considered compliance program in place in the event that something does go wrong down the road.

The aim of such protocols should be to ensure that each decision regarding an intermediary is adequately documented. The documentation should include the nature of the work the intermediary will be performing, and the business justification for engaging this intermediary in the first place. This would include such issues as whether other candidates were considered, whether there are employees in-country who could fulfill the same role, and the expertise and resources the intermediary has to carry out the task. The bribery-related issues pertinent to the task and region should be highlighted, such as how much contact the intermediary will have with government officials; how much business the company does in the region; whether the intermediary has exclusive rights to market the company's products in that territory; and the value of any contract or concession being sought from a government agency. Other factors to consider include how much the intermediary will be paid, whether the payment will be a flat fee or a contingency, and whether the intermediary has represented your company in other countries.

This sort of information can help clarify the degree of due diligence warranted in each case. Can it reasonably be limited to collecting basic personal information and references, conducting a media search, and reviewing prohibited-parties databases, or is a more searching investigation is called for? It can also provide the backdrop against which to evaluate any red flags that do appear. If no likely danger is evident, you will have a record showing that to be the case. If potential issues do appear, the information gathered can serve as a basis for reasoned consideration at higher levels of review within your organization.

At the highest level of review, where the issues are no longer routine or straightforward, you need to be able to base your decision on a full assessment of the relevant circumstances, taking into consideration not only the nature of the assignment and the history of the potential intermediary, but also the balance between your company's tolerance for risk, the urgency of the project, and the possibility of alternative courses of action. This is where real judgment comes into play, and you want the protocols you establish to give you the best opportunity to exercise and document that judgment. You may decide that it's necessary to hold back a project to allow further scrutiny, or you may decide that the situation warrants going forward even in the face of the risks you have identified, but with a rigorous post-contract protocol in place. Either way, faced with a difficult decision, you will know—and will be able to show—that you are acting in an informed, circumspect and deliberate manner, which is all that anybody can ask of you.

Chapter 11
Compliance Tips:
Compliance Training

How to Conduct Compliance Training for 3 Types of Employees

Some companies provide antibribery compliance training because they want to start a dialog with their employees; they hope that broad buy-in from their whole team will translate to good decisions in difficult situations. Other companies train their employees with the expectation, bolstered by the recent Morgan Stanley declination, that their training records will provide a shield should an employee break the law.

Presumably there are still others who, playing the numbers, recognize that the odds are pretty good that they have a nascent bad actor in their midst. Two out of every 100 Americans are under correctional supervision—prison, parole or probation. If you remove children from the corporate calculation (and anyone using child labor has more pressing compliance challenges), the number is closer to three out of every 100. For multinationals with, say, 50,000 employees, that's a sobering statistic.

You can safely assume that your audience for compliance training will include *idealists*, *technicians*, and these *potential bad actors*. Idealists respond to values-based training. They want to talk about both the harm corporations have done in the global community and the good they are capable of doing. They respond well to scenario-based training that leads to lively discussion. This sort of training prepares employees for a broader array of challenges than any compliance professional can foresee; they understand underlying principles and so can apply them as needed. The only risk with this group is that they may be more conservative than necessary, which gives rise to other challenges in corporations established for the primary purpose of generating profit.

The technicians form a smaller, but particularly interesting group. They tend to keep their cards close to their chests. They constitute the ethical majority in your company. Compliance is important, but not central; they want clear, brief training so that they know the answers and can do the right thing. They're often reluctant to engage in "why" discussions and want to head straight to "what": What can they do? What conduct is clearly permitted? What is clearly prohibited, and who can they ask about any grey areas they encounter?

In a subset of the technicians are the contrarians. They end up at the same place, but they want to debate not the rules but the big picture. They ask why corporations should even have to worry about compliance, why the United States is determined to police the world, why this is a priority during a sluggish economy? These are also the participants who groan loudly whenever the person leading the training responds to a question with "Well, it depends." They're not comfortable with ambiguity, they don't particularly like lawyers, and they're probably in a hurry.

The nascent bad actors can be difficult to spot because they're so like the technicians during the course of training. They may not (yet) be actual criminals, of course, but they don't see any inherent value in compliance and they're impatient with discussions of corporate social responsibility and even corporate reputation. There is one in almost every group, and they, too, want bright-line tests and clarity. But in their case, they want this information not to avoid transgression but to evade detection. They favor the "if/then" slippery-slope questions: "If giving a $100 bottle of Scotch is permitted under company policy, then why can't I give a $100 gift card . . . or even cash?" "If we have to use a local contractor anyway, and the customer wants us to use his sister's company, then why doesn't that make more sense than putting the work out to bid?"

The training challenge requires companies to speak to all of these employees at the same time, while giving each group the tools and information they need to make good compliance decisions. Trainers must include enough context to engage the idealists and briefly brave the crossed arms and rolled eyes of the others. Everyone should hear why the company values a strong stance on compliance and the enhanced corporate reputation it fosters. This part of the message can be delivered quickly, with a handful of stunning statistics about the damage done by companies that failed to take their legal commitment and position in the community seriously, as opposed to those that sought to get compliance right even when their competitors did not and when there was no credible risk of prosecution.

Much of the rest of the training session will appeal to the technicians. To keep everyone engaged, if not content, this information can be delivered in scenario format. Describe a situation that is relevant to the company and for which the solution is not too obvious. Participants are encouraged to describe their proposed response to the situation, and then the group can discuss the advantages and disadvantages of the various responses. This not only engages the technicians who are still trying to ferret out the right answer, but enables the trainer to assess whether the message is getting through. A great way to end this portion of the training is with a description of some close calls—situations where employees at other companies were insufficiently conservative and their behavior resulted in corporate investigations, if not enforcement actions.

And then, briefly, you speak to the bad actors near the end. A quick "parade of horribles" is usually sufficient. Give examples of employees who crossed the line when they knew better or failed to seek advice if they were unsure. Show how this approach can prompt a global investigation, resulting in protracted disruption to business, large fines and, for the employees, significant prison sentences.

End with expressions of confidence that this is not that kind of company and that this company is squarely on the right side of the issue. Make sure everyone knows where to get more information if they need it, whether directly or through confidential channels. And always, always stay back for questions at the end of training.

That's when you'll learn the most about your audience and the challenges they face—and what you learn will make you more effective the next time.

Conclusion

Most compliance professionals are drawn to this field not only because it addresses an international crime with devastating consequences, but because it provides new and unexpected challenges. While laws remain fairly stable, the creativity of bribe seekers and bribe payers is almost limitless, so the areas of risk are constantly shifting. We at TRACE are committed to providing tools that support the efforts of these professionals. These include the TRACE Compendium, the TRACE Matrix, our How to Pay a Bribe series, regular benchmarking surveys, and live training events at locations around the world. If you have suggestions for additional topics for future publications, or additional practical compliance tools, we encourage you to contact us.

Made in the USA
Middletown, DE
28 April 2017